Disorderly People

Disorderly People

Law and the Politics of Exclusion in Ontario

Edited by Joe Hermer and Janet Mosher

Fernwood Publishing • Halifax

Royalties generated from the sale of this book will be donated to the Toronto Disaster
Relief Committee.

Editing: Kim Goodliffe
Cover photo: Amy Leang
Cover design: Larissa Holman and Beverley Rach
Production: Beverley Rach
Printed and bound in Canada by: Hignell Printing Limited

A publication of:
Fernwood Publishing
Box 9409, Station A
Halifax, Nova Scotia
B3K 5S3

Fernwood Publishing Company Limited gratefully acknowledges the financial support
of the Department of Canadian Heritage, the Nova Scotia Department of Tourism and
Culture and the Canada Council for the Arts for our publishing program.

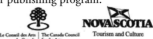

National Library of Canada Cataloguing in Publication Data

Main entry under title:
    Disorderly people: law and the politics of exclusion in Ontario

Includes bibliographical references.
ISBN 1-55266-079-6

1. Civil rights—Ontario. 2. Poor—Civil rights—Ontario.
3. Homeless persons—Civil rights—Ontario. 4. Corrections-Government policy—
Ontario. 5. Ontario—Politics and government—1995-   . I. Hermer, Joe, 1967- II.
Mosher, Janet E. (Janet Eaton), 1958-

KEO819.5.D58 2002   342.713'085   C2001-904276-0

Contents

Acknowledgments

This collection of essays grew from several presentations given at a one-day conference hosted by the Centre of Criminology and the Faculty of Law at the University of Toronto entitled "The Socio-Legal Consequences of the Safe Streets Act" on April 29, 2000. We thank Professor Rosemary Gartner, Director of the Centre of Criminology, and Professor Ron Daniels, Dean of the Law Faculty, for their administrative and financial support in hosting this conference. We are grateful to many of our colleagues and friends who supported this project in a variety of ways: Mary Birdsell, Mickey Cirak, Michael Conner, Shawna Coxon, Rita Donelan, Tony Doob, Jim Phillips, Jamie Piedalue, Peter Rosenthal, John Sewell, Andrea Shier, Mariana Valverde and Jennifer Wood. Thanks also to two anonymous reviewers who commented on the first draft of the manuscript. We are grateful to Wayne Antony at Fernwood Publishing whose enthusiasm for this work was matched only his by extensive patience as we brought this collection together. Finally, thank you to Kim Goodliffe, who edited the manuscript, to Debbie Mathers for typing the final manuscript and to Beverley Rach for designing the book and its cover. Royalties generated from the sale of this book will be donated to the Toronto Disaster Relief Fund.

About the Contributors

Robert Bright is an ethnographer with the Faculty of Medicine at the University of Toronto. His research focuses on strategies of harm reduction, with a particular interest in HIV prevention and injection drug use.

Kelly Hannah-Moffat is an Assistant Professor of Sociology and Criminology at the University of Toronto. She is the author of *Punishment in Disguise: The Governance of Canadian Women's Federal Imprisonment* (University of Toronto Press, 2001) and is co-editor of *An Ideal Prison?: Critical Essays on Women's Imprisonment in Canada* (Fernwood Publishing, 2000).

Joe Hermer is an Assistant Professor of Sociology and Criminology at the University of Toronto. His publications include *Policing Compassion: Begging, Law and Power in Public Space* (forthcoming from Hart Publishing, Oxford in 2002).

Dianne L. Martin is a professor at Osgoode Hall Law School, York University. Before joining the faculty in 1989, she practised criminal law in Toronto for many years. She is the director of the Institute for Feminist Legal Studies, the Innocence Project and the part-time Master of Laws program in Criminal Law. Her writing and research concentrate on issues of criminal justice.

Richard Moon is a professor at the Faculty of Law, University of Windsor. He is the author of *The Constitutional Protection of Freedom of Expression* (University of Toronto Press, 2000).

Dawn Moore is a doctoral candidate at the Centre of Criminology, University of Toronto. Her research interests include drug policy, drug testing, the treatment of drug users in penal settings and the privatization of prisons.

Janet Mosher is a professor at Osgoode Hall Law School, York University, and the Academic Director of the Intensive Program in Poverty Law at Parkdale Community Legal Services in Toronto. From 1989 to 2001 she taught at the faculties of Law and Social Work at the University of Toronto, where she was also the Director of the Combined LLB/MSW program.

Bill O'Grady is in the Department of Sociology and Anthropology at the University of Guelph. His interests focus on marginalized youth, criminology and tobacco control. He received his doctorate in sociology from the University of Toronto.

David Schneiderman teaches at the Faculty of Law, University of Toronto. He was Research Director of the Canadian Civil Liberties Association from 1986 to 89 and later served as Executive Director of the Centre for Constitutional Studies at the University of Alberta. He has authored numerous articles on Canadian federalism and the *Charter of Rights and Freedoms* in addition to editing several books on these topics.

Sue Ruddick is a Professor of Geography at the University of Toronto. She has written extensively on the geography of homelessness in modern cities.

Introduction

Now you can say that I've grown bitter,
but of this you may be sure:
The rich have got their channels in the bedrooms of the poor
And there's a mighty judgement coming
But I may be wrong
—Leonard Cohen, "Tower of Song"

On August 3rd, 2001, the lunchtime news in cities across Canada carried the story of how thirteen people, most of them "squeegee workers," had been convicted in Toronto under the Ontario *Safe Streets Act*. Lawyers for the defendants argued that the Act is unconstitutional, providing police with powers reminiscent of how nineteenth century vagrancy laws were used to punish and imprison the poor. Supporters of the Act, buoyed by the decision at a time when the government had hit a new low in popularity, were able to re-affirm their position that the Act was a legitimate response to questions of public safety and security.

The *Safe Streets Act* is a particularly aggressive example of anti-homeless and panhandling legislation that has become popular in the United States and to a lesser extent in Canada. In the past decade, a number of Canadian municipalities such as London, Oshawa, Ottawa, Halifax, Vancouver and Winnipeg have passed anti-begging and anti-loitering legislation in the form of municipal by-laws. Poverty and civil rights activists have criticized these by-laws as being unconstitutional; in particular that the anti-begging provisions discriminate against poor people and infringe upon their freedom of expression. After a five-year court battle with the National Anti-Poverty Organization, the City of Winnipeg agreed to repeal its by-law that prohibited begging in particular city locations. In agreeing to settle with NAPO, the City confirmed that begging itself posed no harm to people and recognized the full entitlement of the poor to use public space. In the settlement filed in the Court of Queen's Bench, the City acknowledged "the social condition of poverty" in Winnipeg and the entitlement of poor people to be "present," "visible" and "participating" in public spaces and that freedom of expression and equality are "fundamental rights" (Hermer 2001). The City of Vancouver passed an anti-begging by-law two years ago as part of a widespread "civic improvement" campaign. The British Colombia Public Interest Advocacy Centre has initiated a legal challenge to the by-law, which maintains that, like the Winnipeg case, the by-law is an unjustified infringement of freedom of expression, particularly that of poor people. The case is before the courts.

The *Safe Streets Act* represents the first time a modern provincial government has enacted a provincial statute (as opposed to a local municipal by-law) against begging conduct in public space. Indeed, the *Safe Streets Act*, which came into effect on January 31, 2000, was the criminal justice mantelpiece of the re-elected Conservative government of Ontario. Unlike most municipal by-laws, which tend to prohibit alms giving in the most general way (only occasionally using time and place restrictions), the *Safe Streets Act* is both extraordinarily detailed and at the same time vague and sweeping. The two main anti-begging sections of the Act prohibit soliciting in "an aggressive manner" (subsection 2(3)) and soliciting a "captive audience" (subsection 3(2)). Subsection 3(2), under the heading "Solicitation of captive audience prohibited," provides that,

> No Person Shall
> (a) solicit a person who is using, waiting to use, or departing from an automated teller machine;
> (b) solicit a person who is using or waiting to use a pay telephone or a public toilet facility;
> (c) solicit a person who is waiting at a taxi stand or a public transit stop;
> (d) solicit a person who is in or on a public transit vehicle;
> (e) solicit a person who is in the process of getting in, out of, on or off a vehicle or who is in a parking lot; or
> (f) while on a roadway, solicit a person who is in or on a stopped, standing or parked vehicle.

The capricious character of section 3(2) is even more evident when one considers how soliciting is defined in the Act:

> "solicit" means to request, in person, the immediate provision of money or another thing of value, regardless of whether consideration is offered or provided in return, using the spoken, written or printed word, a gesture or other means (section 1).

This definition, which includes the making of a request by *any means*, leaves open the question of whether a visibly indigent person—a homeless person who looks to be in a destitute, desperate state that evokes need and want—would be considered to be soliciting *simply by being present* in the wide array of spaces circumscribed by this section. By their very nature, homeless people have no choice but to "hang around" in public space, attempting to negotiate, as Sue Ruddick argues in this collection, spaces where they can survive and carry out subsistence activities. And while supporters of the Act argue that the spatial specificity of the offence sections do not create a blanket restriction on begging in public space, the reality is that the combined nature of these prohibitions have the effect of broadly covering many of the spaces that homeless people occupy, particularly in the case of sidewalks. This is evident if one thinks of the architecture of public streets: in many stretches of busy urban sidewalks, it would be difficult for a homeless person not to be situated in close proximity to phone booths, taxi stands, parking lots, public transit stops or automated banking machines—all of which are ubiquitous features of streetscapes. And since the Act does not prescribe these places in exact terms, the decision of when someone begging is in the vicinity of these places is left to the discretion of the police officer.

Thus, while the Act details sets of circumstances in which begging is prohibited, a closer look at the text reveals that the detailing in no way defines those circumstances with precision. Rather, the detailing actually constructs a regime that is vague—leaving ample room for discretionary and capricious action—and potentially extremely sweeping in its reach.[1]

Certainly, the very notion of a "captive audience" works to construct the public as vulnerable victims, constantly held hostage in their travels through public by the disorder that anyone begging may embody. More then any other aspect of the Act, this section represents the re-introduction of repealed vagrancy laws that have a disgraceful history of policing the social status of people (see Foote 1956). Status offences target people on the grounds that they are suspicious. As Douglas (1960:13) has pointed out in relation to vagrancy law, policing on the grounds of suspicion is a recipe for discrimination:

> The persons arrested on "suspicion" are not the sons of bankers, industrialists, lawyers, or other professional people. They, like the people accused of vagrancy, come from other strata of society, or from minority groups who are not sufficiently vocal to protect themselves, and who do not have the prestige to prevent an easy laying-on of hands by the police.

In addition to the prohibitions on begging are those that prohibit squeegee work. Subsection 3(2)(d) of the *Safe Streets Act* prohibits, "while on a roadway," the soliciting of a person who is "in or on a stopped, standing or parked vehicle." Furthermore, a section of the *Highway Traffic Act* (subsection 177(11)) was amended to target squeegee workers by prohibiting the conduct of stopping, attempting to stop or approaching a motor vehicle for the purposes of "offering, selling or providing any commodity or service." It is one of the ironies of the *Safe Streets Act* and this amendment to the *Highway Traffic Act* that, despite the government portrayal of squeegee kids as lazy, work-shy troublemakers, the law that they used to target them nevertheless constructs them as commercial solicitors offering an identifiable service to the public.

In the summer of 2000, a coalition of lawyers and social service providers in downtown Toronto encouraged those charged under the *Safe Streets Act* to come forward and be part of a challenge to the legislation. That fall, eighty people charged under the Act were bound together for trial, with their lawyers presenting a defence that the Act was, in a number of ways, unconstitutional. Defence lawyers and the Crown agreed on the facts of thirteen defendants, and the remaining sixty-seven charges were withdrawn. Of the thirteen defendants of *R. v. David Banks et al.* nine were charged under section 3 for "soliciting on the roadway," three were charged under the amended *Highway Traffic Act*, and one was charged under section 2 of the Act for soliciting "in a persistent manner." The circumstances of the defendants, as part of the facts agreed to by the Crown, are revealing: ten of the defendants were homeless at the time of the offences, and three of those charged were squeegee working because they needed food. The circumstances of one defendant is typical of the twelve people who were charged for carrying out squeegee work:

> Mr. B approached a vehicle that was stopped at a red light. He asked for, and received permission to clean the windshield in exchange for money. He cleaned the windshield and left the intersection when the traffic light changed, but did not collect any money. He cleans windshields in order to get money so he can buy food. He is homeless. (Factum at paragraph 5).

The facts were not in issue at the trial; these were agreed to be the parties. Rather, in issue was the constitutional validity of the legislation. Defence lawyers Mary Birdsell and Peter Rosenthal (Factum of the Defence 2000) argued that the *Safe Streets Act*

- constituted an invasion by the province of the Federal government's exclusive jurisdiction over criminal law under the *Constitution Act;*
- infringed upon the right to freedom of expression guaranteed by section 2(b) of the *Charter of Rights and Freedoms* (the Charter);
- infringed upon the life, liberty and security of the person pursuant to section 7 of the Charter by a) denying economic rights necessary for survival and b) by being overly broad and vague penal legislation; and
- infringed upon the right to equality within the meaning of section 15 of the Charter.

The Canadian Liberties Association was granted intervener status to make submissions in relation to the freedom of expression issue. After six months of deliberations, Provincial Court Mr. Justice Babe convicted the thirteen defendants (*R. v. Banks* [2001] O.J. No. 3219). While Mr. Justice Babe accepted defence arguments that the Act infringed upon the defendants' freedom of expression, he found the infringement to be justified under section 1 of the Charter (that is, a reasonable limit in a free and democratic society). He found the limitation on freedom of expression to be reasonable because the Act was intended to protect public "safety." He found no other violations of the Constitution.

In relation to this case, it is important to note that only the sections of the Act under which the thirteen individuals had been charged were under judicial scrutiny. Thus, the most questionable section of the Act, the prohibition of soliciting a "captive audience," is not currently before the court. There is also little known about how this offence section is being used to police visibly indigent people both informally and as part of the 2400 charges that have been laid under the Act as a whole. Nor is there anything known about how many people have been fined or incarcerated under the *Safe Streets Act.*[2]

Certainly the case of *R. v. Banks*, and indeed the *Safe Streets Act*, have been widely portrayed as essentially about the regulation of squeegee work. With respect to the case of *Banks*, this is no surprise, given that twelve of the thirteen defendants were charged for their squeegee labour, under the two offences designed to capture this behaviour. But there is a more significant reason that squeegee kids are widely viewed as being the main target of the Act, and that has to do with how these young people, whose apparent threat to middle-class commuters lies as much in their often unconventional appearance as their conduct, have become figures around which the views about both the efficacy and harms of the radical reforms of the "common sense" revolution have crystallized. Squeegee kids have captured the public imagination as symbols of justification across the political spectrum. Squeegee kids are considered either lazy and often dangerous locusts that take advantage of the public or street smart, entrepreneurial survivors who are the most visible victims of the "common sense" revolution.

Squeegee kids have come to symbolize a certain form of *disorder* that has been central to how and why the government is justified in neo-conservative reforms. A central aspect of how the Ontario government has successfully carried out neo-conservative reforms is through its ability to construct "disorderly people." Squeegee kids, welfare cheats, coddled prisoners, violent youth, aggressive beggars are part of a modern rogues gallery that has been used by the Ontario government to justify sweeping changes in the public character of government. Disorder and the people constructed as embodying disorder have become a central *resource* of political power in Ontario, one that is produced and managed as an essential feature of neo-conservatism across a wide range of government activities.

The law has played a central role in the production of so-called disorderly people and in the facilitation of the forms of economic and social exclusion that these ordering practices have brought. And this role goes beyond the *Safe Streets Act* to include legislation such as the *Safe Schools Act*, the *Parental Responsibility Act* and the *Ontario Works Act*. This legislation has created new forms of regulation and surveillance, involving newly empowered agents, new powers of arrest and search, and harsher modes of punishment. And just as significant is how this legislation has, beyond these instrumental effects, enabled a moral climate where the identification and scapegoating of "disorderly" individuals has become a central role of government. As Dianne Martin argues in this collection, this emphasis on disorder has created a climate where poverty and other expressions of social and economic inequality are translated into narrow questions of criminal justice and law and order. And in carrying out this broad moral campaign, neo-conservatives have been able to effectively occupy a moral "high ground," infused with vague and contradictory notions of "civility," "citizenship," "responsibility," "safety" and "security." Indeed, the underlying logic that has been installed in this politics of exclusion is the forging of a unquestioned linkage between the existence and control of disorderly people and the securing of safety and security. The well being of the public, as constructed by the government, has come to depend upon a mentality of exclusion—that public safety and security depend upon finding, punishing and excluding an enemy "other." Of course, the targeting of disorder is not a phenomenon that is new to the

Ontario government. Indeed, one could correctly argue that the maintenance of "order" has been a historically consistent aspect to the development of a modern police. But what is new and radical about the type of disorder manufactured by the Ontario government is that it is intentionally designed to dismantle both the material and emotional infrastructure of the welfare state. In other words, making up a disorderly set of people has come with an erosion of some of the central principles that have underpinned the democratic and equitable character of our institutions, diminishing the ways in which we are made to feel responsible for each other. And what is most disconcerting about this shift, as it has been carried out in Ontario, is that it has taken place at the very sites in which the government is responsible for some of the most vulnerable and marginalized people in society—those with mental-health issues, the young, the poor and disabled, a disproportionate number of whom are in correctional facilities.

To challenge the politics of exclusion that the Ontario government has deployed, we have assembled a diverse range of authors to explore this neo-conservative landscape. Each of our contributors deploy a different set of lenses, situated from different areas of expertise in law, sociology, criminology and geography, focused on a number of related practices, mentalities and discourses that are part of this politics of exclusion. And while the *Safe Streets Act* has been one of the most visible aspects of this type of neo-conservative politics, the sweep and breadth of reform is not encompassed by just one law or one set of "disorderly people." Thus, the *Safe Streets Act* works as a sort of horizon in this collection, a point from which our authors set out to explore critical sites of the politics of exclusion as they are being played out in Ontario. We hope that this collection makes visible the overall geography of the neo-conservative character of the Ontario government and provides footholds for critique and resistance both within the courtroom and out on the street.

In the first essay of the collection, sociologist Bill O'Grady and ethnographer Robert Bright map out the everyday experiences of squeegee workers, a segment of the homeless population that has been specifically targeted by the *Safe Streets Act* as a disorderly group that must be controlled. Drawing on ethnographic research carried out just before the implementation of the *Safe Streets Act*, they argue that squeegee work provides one of the few types of subsistence activity available to the majority of homeless youth, a form of work that (like other types of employment) provides a level of stability and subsistence. O'Grady and Bright suggest that with the *Safe Streets Act* in place it seems likely that many youth have made themselves "invisible" and may have no choice but to engage in far riskier conduct in order to survive. Implicit in their analysis is the question: whose safety does the *Safe Streets Act* protect?

With squeegee workers having been largely removed from public view, this banishment has been part of the way in which notions of public and private have been reconfigured in the shift to a politics of disorder. In particular, the positioning of the economically disadvantaged (the poor) in relation to both the public and the private has shifted considerably since the election of the Ontario government in 1995. Law professor Janet Mosher explores how two significant legislative reforms (the *Safe Streets Act* and the *Ontario Works Act*) and the administrative practices and discourse surrounding them have combined to shrink both the public and private spaces of the poor. A discourse that portrays the poor as undeserving, lazy, frequently criminal and a threat to public order and safety has been central to both reforms—reforms that operate to remove the poor from public space and public consciousness (entering consciousness only as a perceived threat to safety and order) and simultaneously trample the privacy interests of the poor. Mosher concludes that in sum, "we are witnessing increasing marginalization, the deepening of stereotypes and the exiling of the poor (though citizens) from our political community."

The exiling of the "disorderly" poor from public spaces is taken up by urban geographer Sue Ruddick. Like the doomed Gregor Samsa of Kafka's *The Metamorphosis*, homeless people are suffering a social death that is being accelerated by legislation such as the *Safe Streets Act*. In her contribution, Ruddick attends to the body of the homeless person surviving in the moral geography of a city that has been transformed into a harsh, intolerant landscape. Ruddick argues that this social death is carried out not just through the construction of homeless people as unworthy citizens but through the translation of the gestures of the homeless—such as begging—into "aggressive" acts that, like the insect body of Gregor, should be treated with fear and even revulsion. Underpinning her analysis is a deeply compassionate, morally tolerant vision of the city as a landscape that embraces contradiction, diversity and dissent.

The next two essays provide a detailed analysis of two of the most vital issues having to do with how the *Safe Streets Act* offends the tenets that underlie the constitutional framework that guarantees Canadians certain rights and freedoms as fundamental to the democratic character of Canadian society. In the first essay, law professor Richard Moon considers whether the *Safe Streets Act* prohibits constitutionally protected free speech. Drawing upon jurisprudence from the Supreme Court of Canada, Moon argues that how one characterizes the nature of the speech regulated by the Act is fundamentally important to determining the extent of the Charter protection; political speech, which the court has said lies at the core of the Charter's guarantee of freedom of expression, merits stronger protection than merely "commercial" speech. As Moon points out, in the context of a market-driven, consumerist society the request for money from a passer-by can be glibly portrayed as speech designed to facilitate a commercial transaction. But Moon argues that the exchange is about much more than this; it is an engagement between strangers about need and obligation in our society. For Moon, begging is a profound form of political speech that merits constitutional protection.

David Schneiderman's chapter also raises a question about the constitutional soundness of the *Safe Streets Act*. Legislative competence or jurisdiction is divided between the federal and provincial governments: jurisdiction of the federal government includes the identification and regulation of "criminal" conduct; and of the provincial government, the regulation of streets, sidewalks and highways. Schneiderman argues that much of the *Safe Streets Act* has little to do with regulating the flow of traffic (vehicular or pedestrian) and a great deal to do with regulating behaviour regarded as "disorderly" within the context of a consumerist, market-based culture. It represents, in Schneiderman's words, an expression of disapproval of conduct that crosses the frontier of moral order. As such, the Act is subject to constitutional challenge on the basis that the province is encroaching on an area of federal jurisdiction.

Why has a harsh approach to crime and disorder become a central feature of our culture, particularly in relation to young people? In her chapter, law professor Dianne Martin explores how legislation like the *Safe Streets Act* is part of a widespread "commodification of crime" that rests at the core of neo-conservative politics. For Martin, this movement is particularly disturbing given that it most often targets some of the most vulnerable and marginalized young people living on the street. Martin argues that the commodification of crime and the production of fear has enabled neo-conservatives to re-configure social inequality not as an economic or social crisis but rather as a highly moralized failure of order, one that can be re-policed by expanding, both legally and socially, the realm of those who should be considered criminals.

A key aspect of this commodification of disorder is a renewed appetite for penalty and punishment. Nowhere can this shift to a more punitive mode of governing be seen than in the character of reforms that are re-configuring the area of corrections. In the concluding essay, criminologists

Dawn Moore and Kelly Hannah-Moffat trace the changes that the Ontario government has brought to corrections, changes that invoke two of the most salient themes of the new right: "cutting costs" and "getting tough" on criminals. Carefully refined concepts of rehabilitation and reintegration, which stress the importance of gender, cultural sensitivity and socio-economic factors in decisions made about offenders, have been replaced with policies that stress retribution, deterrence and harsher sentencing and parole strategies. The authors argue that these reforms, which increasingly involve the private sector as part of a push for efficiency, carry out a "penalty of cruelty" that is both irrational and socially destructive.

Joe Hermer
Janet Mosher

Notes

1. The absurd breadth of this section was illustrated by defence lawyers who argued (Factum of the Defence 2000 at paragraph 65) that section 3 of the Act would outlaw
   a) Asking a friend to re-pay a debt as you both leave an automated teller machine (ss.3(2)(a));
   b) Asking a person for change for a dollar as you are waiting to use a public telephone (ss. 3(2)(b));
   c) Asking a person waiting at a bus stop with you for change for a five dollar bill (ss.3(2)(c));
   d) Asking a person to pay his fare on a bus, even if the person asking is the bus driver (ss. 3(2)(d));
   e) Asking a driver waiting to exit a parking lot to pay the charge for parking, even if the person asking is the person employed by the lot owner for that purpose (ss. 3(2)(e));
   f) Asking your spouse for change to put in a parking meter as you exit a car you have just parked while she remains in the car (ss. 3(2)(f)).
2. The Act prescribes the following punishment for sections 2 and 3: a) on first conviction, to a fine of not more than $500 and b) on each subsequent conviction, to a fine of not more than $1,000 or to imprisonment for a term of not more than six months, or to both.

References

Douglas, William O. 1960. "Vagrancy and Arrest on Suspicion." *Yale Law Journal* 1, 3.

Factum of the Defence. 2000. In *R.* v. *David Banks et al.* 2000.

Foote, Caleb. 1956. "Vagrancy-Type Law and Its Administration." *University of Pennsylvania Law Review* 104.

Hermer, Joe. 2001. "Street Act an excuse to outlaw tender hearts." *Globe and Mail.* February 27.

Safe Streets Act, 1999, S.O. 1999, c.8

1.

Squeezed to the Point of Exclusion
The Case of Toronto Squeegee Cleaners

Bill O'Grady and Robert Bright

Introduction

Until recently, many Ontario motorists were regularly approached at urban intersections by small groups of homeless youth with buckets and squeegees in hand, ready to wash their windshields. Squeegee cleaners would normally move towards stopped cars and, with a wave of their squeegee and a nod from a motorist, would then proceed to wash car windshields in exchange for spare change. Squeegeeing, like panhandling, is an income-generating activity that is linked to the homeless population, and in particular, to homeless youth—hence, the popular term, "squeegee kids" (O'Grady et al. 1998; Gaetz et al. 1999; CSPCT 1998). Because of reported incidents of so-called aggressive squeegeeing, but also because of their unconventional and—to some—shocking appearance, squeegiers have been subjected to a great deal of scrutiny by the police, the media, the general public and politicians. The fact that squeegiers actively approach drivers, as opposed to passively panhandling for spare change, makes contact with the homeless unavoidable for many Ontario drivers. Although the public's initial response to squeegee cleaners appeared positive, since the summer of 1995 public reaction and media depictions have been overwhelmingly negative.

The local tabloid press, the *Toronto Sun*, depicted these youth as "herds of locusts who have made it almost impossible for ordinary taxpayers to drive downtown without having their cars descended upon" (*Toronto Sun* 1996a). Specific accusations that squeegee cleaners cause traffic congestion, harass motorists and engage in territorial fights over street corner locations led to 150 monthly summonses issued to squeegiers over the summer of 1996 (*Toronto Sun* 1996b). Then Metro Toronto Chief of

Police, David Boothby, remarked that the problem is "not going to be tolerated" and that legal action is required to combat the problem (*Toronto Sun* 1996c). Local politicians also voiced additional distress about the issue. For example, Liberal MPP Michael Cole, who was reported as having one of his wiper blades damaged by a "squeegee kid," was quoted as saying that he would like to "wipe out street corner squeegee squads in Toronto" (*Toronto Sun* 1996d). Public anxiety over the activity led the former premier of Ontario, Mike Harris, as well as the mayor of Toronto, Mel Lastman, to join in the campaign to rid squeegee-cleaning youth from the streets of Ontario.

The campaign, according to those who wanted to have squeegee cleaning outlawed (the Mayor, the Police Chief, the former Premier, a number of media reporters and some politicians), has been a great "success." Effective January 31, 2000, the *Safe Streets Act* outlawed squeegee cleaning in Ontario. While the Act has not completely removed all squeegee cleaners, the activity has all but disappeared from the streets of Toronto, and there are now only occasional sightings of squeegee cleaners.

Besides anecdotal information and some attention from the press, we know very little about the lives of those who were once involved in squeegee cleaning prior to the *Safe Streets Act*. This lack of research is understandable given the many challenges faced by researchers who seek over a specified time period to keep track of young people who are without permanent addresses and telephone numbers.

This chapter, however, will present an ethnographic account that will provide some insight into the lives of Toronto squeegee cleaners shortly before the time when the activity was legally prohibited by the *Safe Streets Act*. We argue that it would be a mistake to assume that legal control over this activity commenced only after it was outlawed on January 31, 2000. For at least one year prior to the *Safe Streets Act*, particularly during the summer of 1999, police in Toronto were actively involved in an initiative of target policing carried out under the rubric of the Community Action Policing Program (CAPP). Here police were cracking down on squeegee cleaning and other forms of begging conduct that was taking place in certain so-called crime hot spots throughout Toronto. The majority of these so-called crime hot spots were located in the downtown core of the city, an area with a high concentration of hotels, restaurants and upscale retail stores that have a strong tourist presence. The pressure to eradicate squeegee cleaning was well underway prior to the implementation of the *Safe Streets Act*. And it is within this context that in-depth interviews with Toronto squeegee cleaners were undertaken. Our interviews occurred only weeks prior to then Attorney General Jim Flaherty's introduction of legislation that would keep the Ontario government's election promise to give police the power to arrest people for squeegeeing. This chapter will present ethnographic accounts obtained from ten Toronto squeegee cleaners between August 17 and November 1, 1999, about their everyday experiences.

Squeegee Working on the Streets of Toronto

How did squeegee cleaning youth feel about the aggressive policing during the summer months of 1999? Hugh,[1] the oldest squeegier interviewed, had been on and off the streets for twenty years since he left home at age twelve. He had been squeegeeing for seven years, reported that he was active in local community politics and had this to say:

> It's like I'm a second-class citizen. Especially since the crackdown. They've [the police have] gotten worse—they've become more belligerent, more violent ... as long as the cops can go around doing this, it gives people the idea that it's okay to take vigilante tactics on the homeless, on squeegiers, and on gay people too.

When seven other squeegee cleaners were asked their thoughts about the crackdown they generally concurred with Hugh:

> Like right now the police are really bad. And like, they're doing this crackdown ... and the cops are blaming Mel [the mayor of Toronto, Mel Lastman] and Mel's blaming the cops ... Just because you squeegee—I mean you get a guy with a suit and tie walking down the street and they're not going to stop him; but just because we carry a squeegee we get stopped and harassed. Oh yeah, there's squeegiers and panhandlers, they're not just cracking down on squeegiers.
> —Lindsay, a sixteen-year-old homeless female on the streets and squeegeeing for two years.

> At one point I used to like going out and squeegeeing. Now I hate it. 'Cause I'm tired of putting up with people's attitudes ... and there's nothing I can do about it.
> —James, a twenty-two-year-old male on and off the streets for six years, squeegeeing for four years.

Well it's not fair. Why shouldn't we be allowed to do our jobs? I mean we aren't hurting anyone; we're not doing anything wrong. What's wrong with it?
—Wolf, a twenty-year-old homeless male on the streets for six years, squeegeeing for five years.

I don't think that it's fair at all, you know. It's basically like a hate crime, you know—cops are doing this "target policing" thing, and looking at people who look weird or who have squeegees in their hand and then immediately going to them like they're causing all the trouble. I don't think it's fair at all ... we are just trying to live; they're looking at us like we're animals or something, like we're not human beings, and I just don't thinks it's fair at all. Like, cops will come and hassle you and they really know how to intimidate you—scare you into doing things, like confessing and stuff. They're just big bullies. Uh, the police were a lot nicer when I first started. Now they're just rude and they come up to you and they'll shove you around and swear at you and stuff. They're like, really rough. They won't listen to reason and they're just a lot more violent and stuff.
—Lindsay.

About the crackdown.... It's bullshit. Totally bullshit.... For some "jumping squeegiers" [squeegiers who aggressively "jump" stopped cars and clean the windshield without the driver's permission]—squeegiers who harass people—that's fine, send them to jail. But for people who are working hard—honest squeegiers that don't bug people, who ask drivers, who are polite and put up with people's bullshit—I just think that's not right.
—Steve, twenty-three years old, on the streets for eleven years, squeegeeing for nine years.

Well, I think it's a bad thing. I totally think that it's a bad thing. 'Cause the way I'm looking at it [the crackdown] it's illegal—it goes against basic human rights and freedoms. And there are some cops out there who are really evil, but the majority of them are just trying to do their job.
—Brian, twenty-seven years old, on the streets for six years, squeegeeing for three years.

I don't like it. I think it's stupid. We're just out there trying to make a

living honestly instead of doing crime, and they just keep harassing us, throwing us in jail. It costs so much more money to throw us in jail and harass us than to just let us make our money.
—D.R., twenty-three years old, on the streets and squeegeeing for six years.

An issue often discussed was the specific role of the police in enforcing the crackdown. Bubbles, a nineteen-year-old woman who had been squeegeeing for four of her six years on the street, said:

They're assholes. You get the odd nice cop—you get the odd nice cop, like George at Z Division—he's a cool cop. He's the only cop in the City of Toronto who has ever thrown me in jail—but he's a cool cop, though. But ninety percent of them are dicks. Like, you're brought up as a kid and taught that cops are there to help you and "blah, blah, blah" but, through the eyes of a street kid, cops are just there to piss you off. Like, we're just trying to make money and make a living or whatever, because we don't have a job and we don't have a place to live and whatever— yada, yada, yada—and here they are, coming up to us and being assholes and harassing us ... and, like, for no reason! They come around like big dick heads and stuff, and like, freak out on us. If they don't want us there all they have to do is say "Okay, time to move along." They don't have to come along, and like, go [screaming loudly] "Get out of here! Get off the fuckin' road! Rah, Rah, Rah!!" You know? Like, I don't fuckin' want to hear it! They just piss us off and we get mad. It's just a pain in the ass. Oh, yeah, lots of tickets, too. And I've been grabbed by the arm, like, really hard by them, or they'll like, push you down. Or if I'm sitting down they'll grab me by the shirt and pull me up, that sort of thing. Or like, if they want you to get in the car or whatever, they'll just like, push you in ... or they put the handcuffs on really tight, or whatever. They just manhandle you really bad.

Listening to Bubbles' theatrical (and entertaining) description we wondered how much she might be embellishing her account; then, as if on cue, a police cruiser pulled up and one officer yelled at us: "Get off the streets and get a job you pieces of shit!" and drove off.

While Bubbles was more expressive and theatrical than others, these comments reflect what most squeegee cleaners said about their experiences with the police. For two squeegee workers, however, the crackdown was not considered to have increased police attention. Interestingly, those who were less critical of the police were also those who tended to work on the fringes of the downtown core, away from tourists, and dressed in cleaner, more conventional attire. For example Brian, who despite being on the street for six years and living in a squat with no heat or water, was dressed conventionally in popular, brand-name clothes and new roller blades. He had converted to Christianity in the hopes of turning his life around and spent most of his time in church drop-in centres. He said:

> They're level headed. They look at me as a person, not as a rat or a bum on the street. They look at me as an actual person.... I'm polite and I ask [to wash drivers' windshields]. Anyway, they've known me for many years.... They know I don't cause shit ... that I don't sell drugs ... I'm not committing any crimes. I'm just here to live, you know. And that's it.

Another "respectable-looking" squeegee cleaner, James agreed:

> Well to be totally honest with you, I agree with it in a sense ... but in another sense I don't—I think if they're going to cut us off from squeegeeing they should give us another alternative. Right now they haven't done that. And in another way I agree with the crackdown because I mean ... squeegeeing is dangerous. It's dangerous ... and you've got these aggressive squeegiers who don't give a crap. They just don't give a shit about the motorists. I mean, me, personally, I just don't like those kinds of people. They give a bad reputation to me.
> —James, twenty-two years old, off and on the streets for six years, squeegeeing four years, and the only squeegier interviewed with housing.

A few conventional-looking squeegiers who were known to police not to be so-called trouble makers reported little or no problems with police. Two even reported they could squeegee in full view of the police without being ticketed or harassed. Yet those with unconventional hairstyles or clothing (punk style, multi-coloured hair, tattoos and body piercings, ripped-up clothing) were more likely to experience fairly heavy-handed treatment by some police. This differential treatment by police appeared to be based on physical appearances and/or observed behaviours. As James put it:

> I've never had trouble with the police. Never. 'Cause they know—I think the police that work this area, like, they see me and they see that

I'm not bothering people and I'm not jumping cars and stuff—I'm just there to make a quick buck and get the fuck out of there.
[Interviewer:] Do you think the police know most of the squeegiers? Like, do they pick out the ones that cause problems?
Oh, yeah—oh, yeah! Yeah, they know. The cops aren't stupid, right? They can see what's going on.

D.R., a twenty-three-year-old punk rocker with scruffy clothes and dread-locks had been on the streets for seven years. He reports:

Uh, it totally depends on the cop. Some cops are good, some cops are bad. Some of them will talk to us like normal people, others will harass us and make threats. I had this one cop grab me by the throat. Like, we were working at Queen and Spadina and I saw the cops were coming so I said, "Hurry up, the light's changing and the pigs are coming," but I said all this in French. And the cops pulled up and the one just grabbed me by the throat and pushed me up against the wall and threatened to take me down to Cherry Beach and beat me up and stuff, you know? And just because I called him a pig in French.

Several squeegiers reported that police were photographing squeegee clean-ers, taking names down and noting any identifying tattoos, scars or piercings for future reference.

Besides having to deal with the police, many youth experienced problems during interactions with motorists. In fact, all ten youth had many examples of confrontations with motorists. All ten said drivers were often rude and abusive:

I've been flipped the bird [given the finger], I've had oranges and apples thrown at me, uh ... unmentionable stuff thrown at me.... I've been spat at ... um, people getting out of their car and threatening to beat me up.... That's when I just say "I'm here. You're the one who's going to get charged, but I'm here."
—Steve.

People tell you to get a job ... to fuck off ... or they'll turn on their wipers ... run over your foot ... call you a piece of shit ... give you the finger. You name it, they do it. They'll even get out of their cars and grab your squeegee.
—James.

Most squeegee workers dealt with rude or aggressive drivers by ignoring them or simply responding to boorish behaviour by saying "Have a nice day." D.R. told us:

> *I smile and tell them to have a nice day. 'Cause it can't get to me, you can't let it get to you, eh? I just don't let it get to me.... I just sit there and grin. I won't, like, walk away from them—I'll just stand on the curb, stare at them, smile and wave to them, right. Just nice crap.*

Bubbles however mocked offensive drivers:

> *How do I respond to them? I make fun at them. I make fun of them when I'm squeegeeing, like, when I'm out there. I make fun of how everybody says, "no." Like, some of them when you ask them just say "NO!!" and like, I'll make fun of them by standing in front of the car and screaming, "NNOOOOooooo!!!!!" And then there's people that go "No, no, no, no." [waves her finger the way one might scold a pet dog] and I'll like go [crinkling up her nose, and making faces, exaggerating the driver's facial expressions] "No, no, no, no. No squeegee! No, no, no, no!" You just overreact even more than they're overreacting, and then sometimes, they'll laugh about it and give you money anyway.*

Most negative reactions from drivers were rather uneventful, but there were occasions when motorists would react violently. While males tended to report more violent confrontations with irate drivers than the female squeegee cleaners, young women were not immune to such episodes. Visibly shaken, sixteen-year-old Lindsay recounted her experience with an aggressive motorist:

> *Like, yesterday, this guy tried to pull me into his car. Like, he grabbed my hand when I reached to get the change, and he pulled me ... and like, smashed my knee into the door and stuff. It really freaked me out. So I smacked him one ... and so I got away. I don't know who he was, just this middle-aged guy—salesman-looking guy.*

Brian, the conventionally clad, born-again Christian, also reported a serious incident involving aggression with a driver, which ultimately landed him in jail:

> *When that guy bumped me with his car, or when he tried to—well, he*

only bumped me a little bit—well I snapped, and I freaked out and I hit him. Now, even though he shouldn't have bumped me with his car, I still could have walked away. Like, I wasn't hurt—I was angry that he really could have hurt me, you know, that he almost did hurt me. And I was—well, he got out of his car and I could tell he was going to come at me anyway, so I hit him.... But I could use all these arguments [to rationalize my actions].... What I did was wrong. What did they do? They threw me in jail for four and a half months.

While several young people admitted some squeegiers caused trouble and provoked drivers by "jumping" cars, the general picture revealed was of a few "bad apples" whose behaviour received spotlight attention in the media. The majority said they would not even allow aggressive squeegiers to work at their corners. Only two reported, rather sheepishly, that they still "jumped" cars. When these two were asked why they continued to use such tactics they both revealed they had serious heroin addictions, which they needed to deal with on a daily basis to avoid withdrawal symptoms.

Local shop keepers, like the police and motorists, viewed the presence of squeegiers near their stores negatively and saw them as a threat to business:

Yeah, some won't even let us bring a squeegee inside. It's like, why? You let him bring in his briefcase.
[Interviewer]: So, do a lot of businesses discriminate against you?
Everybody, everybody!... A lot of discriminatory bastards! [Imitating a store owner's response to squeegiers]: "Ooh, they're a street kid, and they're dirty and nasty, and have bugs and diseases and stuff." [Pauses.] I think I'm pretty clean—for a street kid, I mean. Like you don't have to be dirty to be homeless. And people criticize me all the time because I look good. It's like: "You think I'm going to give you money when you're dressed like that?"

Many squeegiers spoke of coffee shops and restaurants that refused service to all squeegee cleaners as a matter of policy. Others said shop owners and staff were regularly rude or treated them far differently than other customers. Again, the less conventional looking squeegiers reported more discrimination.

Not only do most of these youth face constant trouble from the police, motorists and the business community, but the amount of money that squeegee cleaners earned just prior to its illegal status was reported by all but one to have declined substantially over the years.

> *Well the best day I ever had I pulled in four hundred dollars. Sometimes you just make a few bucks—like, if it's raining no one needs their windshields cleaned, right? Usually I just pull in twenty or thirty dollars a day, but the most I ever made was four hundred. But that was over three years ago.*
> [Interviewer]: Has it changed much since then?
> *Oh yeah. Like when I first started squeegeeing seven years ago I was pulling in, on average, about one hundred and fifty to two hundred dollars a day. And that was the first squeegee location ever—Queen and Bathurst—okay? But I'd say probably about three years ago things really started to decline, and it's been declining ever since. And the reason is that a few bad apples are giving a bad reputation to all squeegiers.*
> —Hugh.

Steve recalled how lucrative squeegeeing once was for him:

> *I remember nine years ago when I first stepped onto Yonge and Lakeshore here and I made like $480. And I was just like, "Wow!" I paid my rent [laughs] and took the rest of the month off. It was like a fin here, a twenty there—I had no pocket change at all—I had all bills. And I think it was because they [motorists] were impressed at first, like they see someone actually doing something instead of sitting around fucking panhandling or something. Now it's like you're lucky if you get a looney [dollar].*

When James was asked, "Do you think you're making more, less or about the same as three years ago?" he replied:

> *Less. 'Cause I used to be able to make $150 to $200 bucks a day for an eight-hour day. [At the time of the interview he was averaging about $30 per day.]*

Not surprisingly, the significant decline in squeegiers' incomes (beginning about the summer of 1995) parallels the rise in negative public opinion and the increase in negative portrayals of squeegiers in the news media. When homeless youth first adapted this form of income generation, the public's response to them was, if anything, supportive. People expressed such sentiments as, "at least they are trying to do something for themselves and not stealing or sitting on welfare." D.R. singled out the media as the major factor in declining incomes more generally:

> I make a lot less now. Um, right now I'm making a lot less 'cause I'm not doing the drugs. But even when I was doing the drugs I was making a lot less than I was three years ago just because there's a lot more people out there now [squeegeeing]. And there's so much crap in the media, which adds a lot of stress. There's been a lot of bad publicity. Like, I find the media just targets a lot of the bad things and then they just hype it up so much.

Overall, squeegee cleaners reported earning, on average, about fifty dollars a day during the late summer and early fall of 1999. Jack, the one squeegier who reported making over one hundred dollars a day (and doing so consistently) was motivated by his heroin habit and often worked more than twelve-hour days, seven days a week to avoid withdrawal symptoms. (Three other squeegiers reported that the need to support addictions often determined how much money people would make. Those desperate to support addictions worked long hours in all weather, spent most of their money on drugs and were typically in poor health and spirits.) Jack slept on a hot-air vent outdoors, ate infrequently at church drop-ins and agencies, showed visible signs of poor health and hygiene and was fairly depressed. When asked what kept him on the streets and squeegeeing to survive he replied:

> Drugs. That's the whole thing—my whole life is centred around it—the physical addiction. If I don't get it [drugs] I get physically sick, like worse than any kind of flu you could ever have … some really bad sickness. Like you could end up dying from withdrawal—that's why you have to have people monitoring you and stuff, why you have to go to a detox.

Given the range of problems squeegiers face on a daily basis (threats to health and safety, harassment and abuse by police and motorists, declining income), squeegee workers were asked why they continued to squeegee at all. Certainly the activity had lost most of its initial appeal and attractiveness. Yet all ten participants responded unanimously: *the money*.

> The money. The hours. I like that I have no boss, make my own hours, that sort of thing.

Why do I squeegee? ... Because I need the money.

Survival. To get what I need. I don't squeegee every day, I just squeegee for what I need. Sometimes I'll squeegee like every day for a week straight so I can put money in my pockets so the next week I don't have to squeegee. It's a matter of keeping above the poverty line.

Why squeegee? 'Cause I need to survive, and it's the best way for me to get money right now.

Because—this is how I survive. I don't have any place to live, or anything like that, so.... It's just a daily routine that you get used to.

To make money. Just so I can make money like normal people do. I don't like panhandling really, and I'd never do anything like sell my body or do anything sexual. I couldn't do that.
[Interviewer]: So, without squeegeeing, how do you make money right now?
I don't.
[Interviewer]: Do you do anything like shoplift or deal for extra money?
No. I don't engage in criminal activities. I don't have any need for that.

In terms of their futures in general, and in particular, what they expected to do if squeegee cleaning were to be outlawed, these young people really had no clear idea about how they would be making money should squeegee cleaning no longer be an option:

Yeah, if it gets too bad and I have to resort to criminal activity then I will do it—believe me I'll do it.... If they put me in a position where I have no choice, and if I get more desperate than I am now and I have no choice ... then I'll do what it takes to survive.

Hopefully something else will come up. But you never know what's going to happen. I might get a lucky break. I could go on welfare if I wanted—but I'm really anti-government, so I'd be a bit of a hypocrite if I went and got welfare. It's like, I really hate the government, but I'd be living off them ... so like I'd really rather have nothing to do with them.... Or I could get like small jobs, like handing out flyers and stuff.

The future?... I don't really have any plans for making money. Just, uh, whatever—general labour, yeah for like basic money. And I'll get the government to do like, yeah, student loans and welfare and like as much of that as I can. But I'm not adverse to any kind of work, like, whatever it might be.

Maybe carpentry if I can get back into it. I got my papers but I got laid off two years ago. If I could get back into that, that would be cool.

It seems fairly clear that, in spite of the many obstacles encountered in their efforts to earn money from squeegee cleaning and understanding that the work no longer was as lucrative as it once was, squeegee cleaning was still considered to be the best option while surviving on the streets. While paid employment was preferred by most to working on the streets, until that time came—or as one squeegee worker put it "until I get my act together and get off the street"— life as a squeegee worker would continue. Seven of the ten said the key barrier to legitimate employment was the fact they were homeless. Two said their addiction to heroin was the main barrier, and Brian said the lifestyle itself—living on the streets, using drugs and associating with other street people—was the key barrier. Without basic shelter, even the simplest requirements for employment (the ability to wake up and get to work on time, shower and do laundry) become major impediments. Trying to secure housing or employment without these basic needs was generally seen as futile:

When you try to go out and do it on your own, the people you try to communicate with they like, don't listen. Like, I can go try to look at a place to rent, but because I only have one pair of pants, one t-shirt and one pair of socks, I kind of smell a bit. So they don't want to give me a place to live, but without a place to live I can't shower every day. You know what I mean? Like, without a place to live it's very hard to find a job.
—D.R.

Two initiatives were undertaken by the city to address squeegee-youth unemployment: $50,000 dollars was designated by City Council to give a few squeegiers short-term jobs; and the Squeegee Workers Youth Mobility (SWYM) Program was developed to hire up to twenty squeegiers at a time and train them in such things as bicycle repair, jewelry making and web-page design. While well-intentioned, these programs did not address the scope of problems faced by squeegee cleaners) or the sheer number of homeless and unemployed who eke out enough income to survive by cleaning windshields and panhandling. One squeegier, D.R., had been hired through the SWYM Program, and, while he enjoyed the work and training, he summed up the program's effectiveness this way: "It's only twelve hours a week for ten weeks at ten bucks an hour. You know, ten weeks is only two and a half months. Then what do we do? Then we can only go back to squeegeeing. They don't place you in a job afterward or anything."

Exacerbating squeegiers' dilemma of attaining future goals (employment, housing, education) was the marginalizing effect of target policing and the *Safe Streets Act* mandate to "rid the streets" of them (squeegee worker, Hugh). As police pressure increased many squeegiers adopted covert strategies of avoiding police detection and arrest. While working in small teams provided more eyes to spot approaching police, avoiding detection also included migrating from downtown areas (where they had been living under bridges and in parks close to the services they accessed) to remote areas away from the public and away from services. Hugh's description of this migration process adequately portrays the marginalizing effect of target policing on squeegiers:

> *Right now I'm sleeping wherever I can. Last night I slept in the Rosedale Ravine. The crackdown really has us on the run, though. Everyone's like, running around in circles for like, four weeks now. I know I've already got like, seven tickets. The biggest was for $230, supposedly for yelling obscenities in public. That's nothing, though. I know someone who got a $213 ticket for spitting on the sidewalk. The cops are using any and all excuses they can to get rid of homeless people in Toronto. I already know fourteen people who are inside [jail] right now. And they aren't getting out any time soon. What are they in for? Unpaid fines—they can't pay off their fines or pay for bail—but, really they're in there for squeegeeing. This is ridiculous! I mean the police shouldn't be getting away with what they're doing! I mean they're using thug tactics, they're going beyond the law, and I think it's high time that people should organize and fight back.*

Targeting squeegiers with fines and tickets meant squeegiers who could not afford to pay were incarcerated. Most squeegiers reported they would hide their identification and give false names when ticketed to avoid being jailed this way. In addition to fines and tickets squeegiers reported the police went a step further and systematically destroyed any and all squats they could uncover. Under constant threat of arrest and harassment, and after being physically removed from their squats, squeegiers found themselves being pushed further underground into more remote areas. Often these areas were too remote or dangerous for outreach workers to enter, reducing people's contact with badly needed services. Some of these areas also posed significant threats to health and safety: forty to fifty people were living in the Don River Valley flood plain, where flood waters can rise ten to fifteen feet in a matter of minutes; an abandoned warehouse contaminated with PCBs had been home to about fifty people; and a vacant lot known to be contaminated with toxic landfill was home to at least fifty others. Living in secluded areas also increased the risk of violence from other squatters and reduced the chances that someone could intervene.

Conclusion

Despite many squeegiers' commitment to this mode of income generation, less than six months after these interviews took place squeegee cleaning in Toronto had been severely curtailed by police enforcement of the *Safe Streets Act*. While we currently know little about this population there is good reason to believe that many ex-squeegee cleaners continue to be homeless but are surviving with one less economic alternative. We found that the closer we got to the people whose economic behaviour had been targeted and censured, the clearer it was that this activity had been developed as a rational decision to the circumstances faced by those who are young, poor and homeless. Squeegee cleaning cannot be understood apart from this context. Now that the government of Ontario has prohibited this activity, a once distinct segment of the street population is certainly less visible. While this outcome may be perceived by some as a victory over urban squalor and so-called disorder, the prohibition against squeegee cleaning is bound to have undesirable results for both the squeegee workers and society in general.

Many street youth have held more legitimate jobs in the past, but many youth also earn money from drug dealing, petty crime, prostitution, panhandling and social assistance. If squeegee cleaning is eliminated, income options for many street youth are reduced. The problem is exacerbated by the fact that the *Safe Streets Act* severely limits a wide array of begging in public space. Since homeless youth are one of the most socially disadvantaged groups in society, and the government has not put into place alternative forms of employment or social programs, it is very unlikely that this group's income generating patterns have suddenly become more socially desirable, such as paid employment. In fact, given the backgrounds of these youth, as well as the hardships they face on a daily basis, it would not be unreasonable to believe that they will face pressure to earn money in even more precarious sectors of the street economy as long as squeegee cleaning remains unlawful. As squeegee cleaning cannot be done surreptitiously, making it unlawful could force some of these youth to engage in other unlawful activities, such as theft or dealing in drugs, which one can hope to engage in without getting caught.

Our follow-up observations of homeless people over the fall and winter months of 2000–2001 showed that some—typically those who have been chronically homeless—continue to live in remote "out-of-sight" urban areas such as in parks, ravines, wooded lots and fields and under bridges. Having been pushed even further underground by targeted policing and the *Safe Streets Act*, many have left areas where the health and social services they require are accessible, placing them in even more perilous circumstances. And steps to rid the downtown area of "undesirables" may simply have moved them into the parks and wooded areas of "desirable" residential areas.

Moreover, the shift that has taken place in Ontario to censure squeegee cleaning represents a distinct move in policy away from a social welfare model for dealing with homelessness to a model more characteristic of a punitive law-and-order approach. We believe that the adoption of such a crime-control model will further marginalize an already powerless group and could lead to more street crime. This seems to be the case in Vancouver. The street youth culture in Vancouver during the early 1990s was, and perhaps continues to be, characterized by greater problems relating to street crime and drug use than was the case in Ontario prior to the *Safe Streets Act* (Hagan and McCarthy 1997). In Vancouver the police have traditionally played an important role in attempts to control street youth through vigilant surveillance and charging practices. This so-called law-and-order approach to street crime in Vancouver appeared to exacerbate urban youth problems: Vancouver street youth were found to be younger, involved in more crime and more serious crimes generally, used more drugs and harder drugs and came into contact with the criminal justice system at younger ages than Toronto street youth. On the other hand, until recently, the primary ways of dealing with street youth in Toronto had fallen under the social service delivery system (counselling, drop-in centres, etc.). With the *Safe Streets Act*, this has now changed, and it seems likely that, as in the case of Vancouver, the lives of homeless youth will become more fraught with the dangers of having to survive on the street.

The act of censuring squeegee cleaning in Ontario can be interpreted as being part of a more global phenomenon. In other parts of Canada, and in the United States and England, recent years have been witness to more and more legal controls being targeted against the poor. The ever expanding activities of the criminal justice system, persistent cutbacks to social spending, sky rocketing costs of housing in large urban centres and growing gaps of income inequality show us that society is becoming more exclusive (Young 1999). The reaction to squeegee cleaning in Ontario is a clear example of how a marginalized and relatively powerless group is being squeezed to the point of exclusion.

Note

1. Pseudonyms have been used for all interview informants.

References

Community Social Planning Council of Toronto (CSPCT). 1998. "Surviving the Streets."

Daily, G. 1996. *Homeless: Polices, Strategies, and Lives on the Street.* New York: Routledge.

Gaetz, S., B. O'Grady and B. Vaillancourt. 1999. "Making Money: The Shout Clinic Report on Homeless Youth and Employment." Toronto: Central Toronto Community Health Centres.

Hagan, J., and B. McCarthy. 1997. *Mean Streets.* Cambridge: Cambridge University Press.

O'Grady, B., R. Bright and E. Cohen. 1998. "Sub-employment and Street Youths: An Analysis of the Impact of Squeegee Cleaning on Homeless Youths." *Elsevier Security Journal* 11.

Rossi, P. 1989. *Down and Out in America: The Origins of Homelessness.* Chicago: University of Chicago Press.

Toronto Star. 2000. November 28.

Toronto Sun. 1996a. August 19.

_____. 1996b. June 21.

_____. 1996c. July 20

_____. 1996d. June 21

Webber, M. 1991. *Street Kids: The Tragedy of Canada's Runaways.* Toronto: University of Toronto Press.

Young, J. 1999. *The Exclusive Society: Social Exclusion, Crime and Difference in Late Modernity.* Thousand Oaks, CA.: Sage.

Zdanowicz, Y.M., et al. 1993. "Views From The Street: Conducting Research with Street Youth." Toronto: Addiction Research Foundation.

2.

The Shrinking of the Public and Private Spaces of the Poor

Janet Mosher

Introduction

Massive reforms to various federal and provincial social policies over the past decade have significantly re-shaped both the physical and ideological landscape of poverty. The day-to-day realities of living in poverty have become harsher; in Ontario for example, welfare benefits have been cut by 21.6 percent, eligibility criteria have been tightened, workfare has been introduced and the discourse (the language and text used to construct knowledge) of welfare fraud and the practices connected with its detection have led to increased scrutiny and surveillance of recipients. Police have been given new powers to remove from the streets panhandlers and squeegee workers, who, like welfare recipients, have been demonized as a threat to public order and safety. In what follows, I examine how the economically disenfranchised (the poor) have been re-positioned in relation to the private and the public within this shifting landscape. I consider in particular the impact of two recent legislative reforms in Ontario, the *Ontario Works Act (O.W.A.)* and the *Safe Streets Act (S.S.A.)*. Although my focus is Ontario, similar legislative reforms have occurred throughout many jurisdictions in North America.

The Public/Private Divide

The public/private divide occupies a central place in liberal thought. The relationship between the public and the private is often understood, and played out, in a deeply dichotomous way. The public is configured as the antithesis, or opposite, of the private. Particular attributes are associated with each, and these attributes themselves are often paired in similarly dichotomous ways. So, for example, the public/private split is often applied in relation to work and family; work as public, family as private. Associated with work are the attributes of competitiveness and independence; with the family, nurturance and dependence. The values of one are assumed to be incompatible with the other realm or sphere. Thus, the general structure of the categorization is one in which there is a solid and bright line separating two spheres of life and of activity.

As many others have illustrated, when this general categorization structure is used to delineate actual activities, spaces and practices it is applied inconsistently, creating a great deal of ambiguity (Brett 2001; Pitkin 1981). So, for example, it is very common to hear the market (the paid world of work) described as public in relation to the (private) family but as private in relation to the (public) state. Moreover, an extensive body of scholarship has demonstrated the falseness of the assumed separation of spheres of activity—the market for example is dependent upon the care provided in the domestic realm—and has shown how the assumed separation contributes to the devaluation of the unpaid labour women perform in the home.

Notwithstanding the many ambiguities in relation to the use of the terms public and private, I agree with Nathan Brett's suggestion that in most uses of the terms, a particular normative structure can be identified (Brett 2001). The norms identified with the term private are those of exclusion and partiality; those associated with the term public are those of fairness, equality and impartiality. This essay develops the concepts of private and public more fully and then considers how the poor are being re-positioned in relation to each.

The Private

The norm of exclusion has long been, and continues to be, central to the concept of the private. In relation to property, private property vests in the owner exclusive rights to possession—to control who, if anyone, shall have access. More recently, especially in relation to the notion of a right to privacy, the ability to control access not only to one's home but also to one's body and to information about oneself have been identified. This ability to keep others out is, in turn, understood to be centrally important to the values of dignity, autonomy and freedom. This notion of privacy as exclusion has, for example, animated the decisions of the Supreme Court of Canada. It is significant to note that while the *Canadian Charter of Rights and Freedoms* does not expressly confer a right to privacy (nowhere in the Charter is this language used), the Supreme Court has found that such a right is implied by both section 8 (the right to be secure against unreasonable search and seizure) and section 7 (the right not to be deprived of life, liberty or security of the person except in accordance with the principles of fundamental justice). The case of *R.* v. *Dyment* (1988) is illustrative of the Supreme Court's approach to the concept of privacy.

Dyment had been rendered unconscious in an automobile accident and taken to hospital. Without his consent, the treating physician collected a vial of blood for medical purposes. The physician subsequently gave the vial to a police officer. An analysis of the blood sample revealed Dyment to have been intoxicated. Dyment argued that his right to be secure against unreasonable search and seizure had been violated and that the evidence (the blood analysis) should be excluded, an argument that the Court accepted.

The Supreme Court of Canada noted that in earlier cases it had identified privacy as the core interest protected by section 8 and then proceeded to elaborate more fully than in past decisions a conception of privacy. The Court, referencing Alan F. Westin's book, *Privacy and Freedom,* noted that "society has come to realize that privacy is at the heart of liberty in a modern state ... grounded in man's [sic] physical and moral autonomy, privacy is essential for the well-being of the individual" (*Regina* v. *Dyment* 1988: para. 17). Significantly, the Court also accepted the notion that was articulated in a report by a Department of Justice Task Force (*Privacy and Computers*) of zones of privacy: the territorial or spatial; those related to the person (more specifically the body); and those that arise in the information context (*Regina* v. *Dyment* 1988). In relation to the territorial or spatial zone of privacy the Court, as in its earlier decision in *Hunter* v. *Southam*, noted the historical tendency to think of privacy solely in relation to property, especially the home. The Court rejected this narrow conception of privacy, quoting Westin's observation that, "to protect privacy only in the home ... is to shelter what has become, in modern society, only a small part of the individual's daily environmental need for privacy" (*Regina* v. *Dyment* 1988: para. 20). The acceptance of this proposition also led the court to view privacy as linked to the human body and in this regard, the Court reasoned that privacy protects the dignity in the human person and transcends the physical body. The notion that the dignity of the human person transcends the physical leads readily to the third aspect of privacy identified by the Court—the control of information about oneself. The Court, quoting from the Task Force, observed that this dimension of privacy flows, "from the assumption that all information about a person is in a fundamental way his [sic] own, for him [sic] to communicate or retain for himself [sic] as he [sic] sees fit" (*Regina* v. *Dyment* 1988: para 22).

In other Supreme Court cases, as in *Dyment*, the notion of privacy at play is grounded in the norm of exclusion. The Court has moved well beyond the historical association of privacy and property to embrace the ability to control access to one's body and to personal information. The ability to be able to control access to each of these dimensions has been identified by the Court as absolutely crucial to human dignity and autonomy. And as articulated by the Court, it is the right to privacy that creates the shield one can uplift to prevent others from transgressing these boundaries without consent.

Brett argues, correctly in my view, that the designation of a sphere or activity as private often connotes not only exclusion but also partiality. By this he means that within a realm of activity or interaction identified as private it is widely accepted that those within that defined realm may justifiably act partially toward one another; that is, like cases may be treated differently (Brett 2001: 8). An example that he uses is that of the family; it is widely accepted that within the private family one may act partially towards other members of the family. That is, one would not be morally condemned for attending to the needs and interests of, for example, one's own children, over the interests of other children.

I think it fair to suggest that at least to this point in my discussion, privacy has been portrayed in a very positive light, something which reasonable people would desire to have in their lives. And as I develop later in the paper, the fact that privacy is not equitably distributed across society (some enjoy a great deal more privacy than others) represents an injustice. Yet, notwithstanding the positive aspects of privacy—of this right to be left alone—the concept of privacy simultaneously operates in ways that perpetuate disadvantage. Elizabeth Schneider's article, "The Violence of Privacy" names the concern in its title (Schneider 1991). What Schneider and many other feminists have noted is that privacy is often invoked by the state as a justification for non-intervention. So, for example, the characterization of the family as private was (and to some extent still is) used as an explicit justification for non-intervention by the State in situations where men abuse their intimate partners. Because the privacy interest was ascribed to the family, it was the family that had the right to be left alone; to be free from government intervention. Of course, in most instances, this simply served to reinforce in families the power of abusive men—those who were indeed, in control.

Additionally, notions of privacy are readily linked to individualistic, libertarian conceptions of autonomy that lay the blame for unemployment and poverty at the feet of individuals, not social structures. And finally, as Brett suggests, shifts in the categorization of particular space, activities or things from public to private often signal growing inequalities, a point which, as discussed below, is amply illustrated by the *Safe Streets Act.*

The Public

Let me begin by returning to Brett's suggestion that the norms underlying the concept of public are fairness, impartiality and equality. While I agree with Brett that these are often the norms articulated in relation to domains or activities designated as public, frequently the norms are not respected in practice. Moreover, there are instances where the designation of public is meant to capture simply the idea that all or most in a given community are affected and has nothing at all to do with the norms of fairness or impartiality.

To name a space or property as public is then to suggest that it is governed by norms of impartiality, equality and fairness. This does, I think, conform to our common expectations about public space as (relatively) open to all: streets, sidewalks and parks for example. To use Waldron's words, public spaces are ones that "anyone in the society [may] make use of … without having to secure the permission of anybody else.… In the broadest terms, they are places where anyone may be" (Waldron 1991: 297–98).

A further significant sense in which the concept of the public is often used relates to the notion of public life and the democratic process. Envisioned in this use of the public is an ongoing and vigorous process of discussion and debate about matters of collective concern in which all members of the community participate. Pitkin speaks of this as "public life"; the "possibility of shared, collective, deliberate, active intervention in our fate" (Pitkin 1981). Here is one instance where, although the articulated norms are fairness, impartiality and equality, in historical practice entire segments of the population have been excluded from the so-called public (women and aboriginal peoples for example).

The Poor in Relation to the Private

For those who are without a home, privacy rarely operates as a shield they can uplift to keep uninvited others out. The homeless have no space to which they can control access; rather they constantly brush up against the private property claims of others, which are used to exclude them and to deny them shelter, warmth and comfort. And without a home, many private functions associated with the home (sleeping, bathing, eating) must be performed in public places, visible to anyone who cares to look.

Those who are recipients or beneficiaries of welfare also experience little privacy. This arises not because they have no home (although their accommodation may be so crowded as to reduce their privacy) but because of the intense scrutiny of virtually every detail of their lives; a scrutiny that has dramatically intensified since the 1995 election of the Conservative government.

One of the most fundamental reforms enacted by the Ontario government was to introduce into the general regulations of the *Ontario Works Act (*O.W.A.*)* a new definition of spouse, first in 1995 and again in 2000. The origins of present-day welfare legislation in Ontario can, in part, be traced historically to mother's allowance. Single mothers (later single parents) were (and continue to be) eligible for benefits. But the important catch here is the word single—when is one single for the purposes of determining welfare eligibility? For a long period of time in the administration of welfare, a great deal of attention was focused upon catching men in the homes of women who were receiving benefits as single mothers. If there was a man in the house, it was assumed to be his responsibility—not the state's—to provide for the woman and children in the house. It did not matter whether he was in fact providing for them, nor whether he had any legal obligation to do so. Because women's initial, and continuing, eligibility for benefits depended on the absence of men in their homes, women's lives became subject to intrusive investigations and often to the arbitrary or capricious termination of benefits. Often, the determination that a woman was not, in fact, single turned upon whether the welfare investigator concluded there was a sexual relationship (Little 1998). For a short period of time (1987–1995) the definition of spouse for welfare purposes was amended to conform to the family law definition. Importantly, this meant that a woman and man could form a relationship, and even co-habit for up to three years, before a determination would be made that they were a couple. But the definition of spouse introduced in 1995 largely returned to the state of things before 1987; persons of the opposite sex residing in the same dwelling place were presumed to be spouses. The 2000 amendment expanded the definition of spouse to include same sex partners.

As part of the application process, and periodically once in receipt of benefits, applicants are required to complete a lengthy questionnaire about their spousal status. Applicants are required to answer questions about everything from how and with whom they spend their leisure time, to who prepares and shares in their meals. So, for example, the questionnaire includes these questions: Who eats meals with you at home? Does your co-resident ever do your laundry (or the children's)? Does your co-resident attend your children's birthday parties?

In addition to having to provide a vast amount of personal information, the O.W.A. and regulations authorize the gathering of information about an applicant or recipient from others. An Eligibility Review Officer (ERO) is empowered by the Act to enter, without a warrant, any place other than a dwelling if he or she has reasonable grounds to believe that there may be evidence relevant to determining a person's eligibility for benefits. EROs are empowered not only to enter premises, but to inquire into all matters relevant to their investigations, and to demand the production of anything deemed relevant to their investigations. With a warrant, EROs are empowered to enter a dwelling house to search for evidence relevant to eligibility (subsection 65(1) *O.W.A.*). But additionally, the regulations authorize home visits; with or without notice a visit (a euphemism for a search) may be requested to verify initial and ongoing eligibility (section 12 Regulation 134/98 *O.W.A.*). The "search" is limited to only those things in plain view. A refusal to permit the visit will result in the denial or termination of benefits, unless the refusal was for good reason (of course, what constitutes a good reason is *not* determined by the applicant/recipient).

Even more sweepingly, an applicant is required to sign a consent form, consenting to the disclosure of information (by virtually anyone having information about the applicant). These so-called consents (in practice there is little that is voluntary about them since benefits can be denied if the consents are not signed) are then used to garner information from child welfare authorities, from addiction counsellors, from employers and a host of others who have often been entrusted with deeply personal information about the applicant (section 19 Regulation 134/98 *O.W.A.*).

In addition to these legislative and regulatory provisions it is imperative to consider the discourse that has surrounded and supported these reforms. This discourse portrays welfare recipients as lazy, unmotivated, promiscuous (in the case of women), deceptive and undeserving (Evans and Swift 2000). Much of this stereotype has been constructed through the constantly invoked (yet empirically false) claim of widespread welfare fraud and the government's vow of zero tolerance of it (Morrison 1998). Very shortly after coming to power in 1995, the Conservative government introduced a province-wide, 1-800-welfare-fraud hotline to encourage people, under a cloak of anonymity, to report suspected fraud. The province created a new central fraud prevention team, gave local welfare offices the power to create their own and promised taxpayers savings in the order of $100 million in the first year.

The stepped-up campaign to eradicate welfare fraud has meant that the state has been more actively seeking to locate men in the houses of single women on welfare (and now, in light of recent reforms to include same-sex partners, men in the homes of men, women in the homes of women). And in addition to the techniques of surveillance reviewed earlier—the home visits, spousal questionnaires, etc.—welfare fraud discourse and devices like snitch lines draw a huge array of others into the role of surveillance. Landlords, neighbours, children's teachers and a multitude of others who may have evidence relating to intimate aspects of recipients' lives are questioned and/or come forward voluntarily (wanting to help end the fraud that they have been led to believe is rampant) (Little 1998: 164). One very significant implication of this is that it becomes virtually impossible to keep private the fact that one is in receipt of welfare. This has tremendously important repercussions because of the stereotyping and widespread discrimination to which recipients—and their dependents (children)—are subjected. As Josephine Grey notes, "When you live on social assistance, you live in Stalinist Russia—your neighbour, your [social] worker, even your friend might report you. You live with all kinds of terrorist fears" (Little 1998: 164).

In light of this, what might we say about how welfare recipients are positioned in relation to privacy? The ability to control access to one's space or territory is clearly curtailed by home visits; an agent of the state can simply drop by, unannounced if he or she chooses, for a so-called visit. Although strictly speaking an applicant/recipient can refuse (and thus control) entry, in fact he or she has little choice, since a refusal may well lead to the denial or termination of benefits.

One's body also becomes the object of surveillance and scrutiny—and in particular, scrutinized as to whether that body is intimately connected to another. As noted, this surveillance is carried out not only by the state but by landlords, neighbours and others who look for evidence of spouses in the houses of persons they believe to be welfare recipients. In this context of intense scrutiny, one hardly enjoys "the right to be left alone."

With respect to the informational plane, it is clear that here too welfare applicants/recipients have little, if any, control over personal information about themselves. Intensely intimate details of their lives and relationships are garnered not only from applicants/recipients generally but as noted, from a host of others. The powers of the state to collect personal information are sweeping; in this domain as well, an applicant/ recipient hardly enjoys privacy. There is ample evidence that trust, dignity, self-esteem and autonomy are undermined by the routine invasions of privacy that characterize the welfare system (Little 1998; MacFarlane 1995).

Taken as a whole, the legislative framework, the policies, the practices and the accompanying discourse operate to construct the poor as persons who don't deserve to be in control of anything; rather they are persons who need to be controlled, disciplined and reformed by others. Single mothers in particular represent disorder, since they stand outside the structure of both the hegemonic nuclear family and often, the labour market. Welfare recipients, and especially single mothers, are constructed as persons who ought not to possess any expectation of privacy; they are, in effect, cast as objects, to be reformed by the "public" for the betterment of the "public." Thus, privacy is preserved for others, for the economically privileged. And note too that the "public" is one from which they are plainly excluded. Rather, they are positioned as its opposition.

Let me briefly note here that I have not engaged issues related to the constitutionality of these various welfare reforms. Rather I have used some of the Supreme Court decisions on privacy in other contexts in order to flesh out more fully the meaning ascribed to privacy in contemporary Canadian society. But there are important constitutional questions about whether, for example, home visits constitute an unreasonable search under section 8 of the Charter and about the permissible scope of information demands on someone who seeks benefits from the state. The only component of the welfare reforms that I have described that has been litigated is the definition of spouse introduced in 1995. In a judgment delivered in the spring of 2000 (and now on appeal to the Ontario Court of Appeal) the Divisional Court found the new definition to violate section 15 of the Charter (the equality rights guarantee). In the course of its judgment the Court acknowledged and condemned the widespread stereotyping of, and discrimination against, single mothers on welfare. And the Court stated that, "the serious invasion of their [single mother's] privacy and the unwarranted assumption of their dependence upon a man occasioned by the legislation can only reinforce this unfortunate aspect of their lives" (*Falkiner* 2000: para. 124). Thus, at least on one occasion, a Court has been prepared to acknowledge the "serious invasion" of welfare recipients' privacy.

One can also see the negative side of the concept of privacy at play in relation to welfare policy itself. The notion of the right to be left alone, to be in control, is fully compatible with a deeply conservative political agenda. The *Ontario Works Act* includes in section 1 the following statement of purpose; the Act is to "establish a program that: a) recognizes individual responsibility and promotes self-reliance through employment; b) provides temporary financial assistance to those most in need while they satisfy obligations to become and stay employed; c) effectively serves people needing assistance; and d) is accountable to the taxpayers of Ontario." As I have noted elsewhere, a clear premise of the legislation is that poverty is rooted in the failure of individuals rather than arising as an inevitable consequence of a market economy (Mosher 2000). As with intimate abuse in the family, the dichotomy of public/private is invoked both to obscure the role of the public state in maintaining the conditions that create unemployment and destitution and to deny that the state has any obligation to intervene. Rather, it is individuals who are responsible, who are in control of their destinies.

The Poor in Relation to the Public

As noted above, much of the discourse surrounding recent welfare reforms has constructed the poor as undeserving, lazy and frequently criminal. In addition, the discourse and practices have positioned the poor in opposition to the public. The poor loom as dangerous, menacing others who stand outside the existing order and who share little, if anything, in common with the hard-working taxpayer. This discourse has also facilitated a second significant legislative reform, the *Safe Streets Act*, which prohibits the performing of particular activities in public spaces. As pointed out elsewhere in this collection, while the Act does not specifically name the homeless, the poor, the beggar or the squeegee worker as the objects of its regulation, it is clear that these are the persons who will, in fact, be regulated. The activities prohibited are those most often associated with persons in dire financial need. For example, it prohibits requests or gestures for money from persons "using, waiting to use or departing from automated teller machines," from persons waiting at a taxi stand or public transit stop, or from persons who are in or on a stopped, standing or parked vehicle. Significantly, then, the Act regulates the use of public spaces in ways that proscribe the activities of those who are economically marginalized.

In banning these activities the Act has gone a considerable distance toward removing particular persons (beggars, squeegee workers) from public spaces. In Toronto this has been most acutely visible in relation to squeegee workers. Prior to the Act, squeegee workers were regularly present at major intersections throughout the city; subsequent to the Act they have been displaced from these highly visible spaces.

It is important to consider what is happening in this form of regulation of spaces that we have long considered public. Collins and Blomley have suggested that the proliferation of anti-panhandling by-laws and statutes across the country can be understood as part of an effort to purify the urban landscape, to create the right image to attract both domestic, middle-class consumers and international capital (Collins and Blomley 2001). If this is right, then it is fair to characterize this form of regulation as privatization; the norms of partiality (the interests of the middle and upper classes are preferred and protected) and exclusion (of the economically marginalized) are both present. The shift away from the norms associated with the public and toward those associated with the private does mark, as the earlier comments of Brett suggested, increasing inequality.

As with welfare reform, the reform of the streets has been undertaken in the name of the public, with the express goal of making the streets safe for the public. But this is not an inclusive public; the streets are not being made safe for those who are actually threatened on the streets, the homeless. So, though the word public is used, it refers to a gentrified public indeed.

Finally, if we consider the sense of the public as meaningful and engaged debate and discussion in which all members of the community participate, the implications of the Act are profound. It is no doubt true that we do not live in a society where there is lively debate about important political issues occurring regularly on our streets or in our parks. And it may well be that many of our exchanges with panhandlers or squeegee workers do not involve intense political discussions (although some clearly do). Yet the presence of panhandlers and squeegee workers on our streets serves a deeply important function. Their presence, at least for many, spurs important questions about why and how so many people could be so destitute; about how existing policies and practices might be contributing to this; about how others (oneself included) benefit from existing arrangements; and about the nature of our obligation to strangers in need. The removal of the survival activities of the poor from our streets facilitates, for those of us who are economically privileged, a ready slip into a self-comforting belief that all is well.

A personal example may help to illustrate this point. Prior to the *Safe*

Streets Act squeegee workers often cleaned the windshield of my car as I was driving my five-year-old daughter to or from school. On many occasions we used those moments to talk about poverty, homelessness and our responsibilities to each other. On one occasion the squeegee worker who cleaned our windshield thanked me for the money and said that now he had almost enough money to buy a birthday cake to celebrate his birthday. My daughter was struck by this, in fact, quite outraged by the reality that someone wouldn't have enough money for a birthday cake. We talked at length about the many things many people don't have and what we might do about it. For several months now, since the enactment of the *Safe Streets Act,* there have been no squeegee workers at the intersections where we had come to expect—indeed rely—upon them. And while, of course, I can still talk to my daughter about poverty and homelessness, these issues have clearly become less visible, immediate and compelling to her (and no doubt to a great many others).

Conclusion

Taken together these two legislative reforms—not to mention all of the other contributing features of our present landscape—have the effect of shrinking both the public and private spaces of the poor. Those who are poor and on the street, or poor and receiving welfare, are denied their privacy. They are constructed (portrayed and represented) as "others," as persons who stand outside of, and thus constitute a threat to, the existing order. As such, they are persons who are seen to have no legitimate expectations of privacy that need to be respected. The zones of privacy (of territory, of body and of home), which are so fundamental to dignity and autonomy, look very different for the economically privileged and the economically marginalized; privacy is *not* distributed equitably. The economically marginalized are rarely in the position of being able to claim their privacy in order to keep others from transgressing the boundaries that they do not want crossed. To the contrary, the State and many citizens feel entitled to transgress these boundaries with absolute impunity. This "othering" of the poor is also used to exclude the poor from the so-called public: from public space, from public debate, from public consciousness (entering consciousness only as a perceived threat to safety and order). In sum, what we are witnessing is increasing marginalization, the deepening of stereotypes and the exiling of the poor (though citizens) from our political community.

References

Brett, N. 2001. "Inequality and the Divisions between Public and Private: Reflections on Privacy, Patents and Biotechnology." Paper prepared for the Law Commission of Canada, Legal Dimensions Initiative 2001.

Collins, D., and N. Blomley. 2001. "Private Needs & Public Space: Politics, Poverty and Anti-Panhandling By-laws in Canadian Cities." Paper prepared for the Law Commission of Canada, Legal Dimensions Initiative 2001.

Evans, P., and K. Swift. 2000. "Single Mothers and the Press: Rising Tides, Moral Panic, and Restructuring Discourses." In S. Neysmith (ed.), *Restructuring Caring Labour: Discourse, State Practice, and Everyday Life.* Toronto: Oxford University Press.

Falkiner v. *Income Maintenance Branch.* 2000. Ontario Divisional Court. File No.557/98.

Little, M. 1998. *'No Car, No Radio, No Liquor Permit': The Moral Regulation of Single Mothers in Ontario, 1920–1997.* Toronto: Oxford University Press.

MacFarlane, E. 1995. "No Lock on the Door: Privacy and Social Assistance Recipients." Appeal 1.

Morrison, I. 1998. "Ontario Works: A Preliminary Assessment." *Journal of Law and Social Policy* 13.

Mosher, J. 2000. "Managing the Disentitlement of Women: Glorified Markets, the Idealized Family, and the Undeserving Other." In S. Neysmith (ed.), *Restructuring Caring Labour: Discourse, State Practice, and Everyday Life.* Toronto: Oxford University Press.

Pitkin, H. 1981. "Justice: On Relating Private and Public." *Political Theory* 9.

Regina v. *Dyment.* 1988. Supreme Court Reports 2.

Schneider, E. 1991. "The Violence of Privacy." *Connecticut Law Review* 23.

Waldron, J. 1991. "Homelessness and the Issue of Freedom." *University of Southern California Law Review* 39.

3.

Metamorphosis Revisited:
Restricting Discourses of Citizenship

Sue Ruddick

As Gregor Samsa awoke one morning from uneasy dreams he found himself transformed in his bed into a gigantic insect. He was lying on his hard, as it were armor-plated, back and when he lifted his head a little he could see his dome-like brown belly divided into stiff arched segments on top of which the bed quilt could hardly keep in position and was about to slide off completely. His numerous legs, which were pitifully thin compared to the rest of his bulk, waved helplessly before his eyes. What has happened to me? he thought.
—From *The Metamorphosis* by Franz Kafka

Introduction

So the story begins by Franz Kafka, about a man who suffers a *social death* and then a real death largely through mis-recognition and neglect. Samsa first tries to resist this transformation, then eventually accommodates these deaths in a profound state of alienation. More horrifying than the actual physical transformation of Samsa is the profound suffering he endures as every gesture, every attempt at communication is met with revulsion. In the final paragraphs of the story depicting his demise, his family rereads his gestures, not as a quest for recognition but as an act of violence, ultimately justifying their complicity in his death.

The *Safe Streets Act*, enacted in Ontario, Canada, on January 31, 2000, marks a similar transformation, denoting not simply another slide in the painful, incremental social death of homeless people but marking more generally the metamorphosis of civic life itself in this province. Known popularly as the "Anti-Squeegee Act" this legislation re-interprets the gestures and acts of homeless people, whether begging on the sidewalk or squeegeeing car windows, as acts of aggression.

What I would like to do in this article is revisit the geography of the Act in its larger context at a variety of spatial scales. The Act changes social relations across the province, but the Act also has impacts on a range of spatial scales: the neighbourhood as police use it to target particular areas for "cleanup"; particular streets that represent the intersection of "prime" and "marginal" spaces (see section entitled The Moral Geography of the City); and at the level of the body in the ways that simple gestures are reinterpreted. First, I would argue that, like the metamorphosis of Gregor Samsa, the Act must be read as a marker in a long line of events contributing to the social death of homeless people in Ontario. Second, although the Act is province-wide, it inscribes itself in a particular geography of social life, acting at the scale of the body, the street and targeting key locations in the downtown cores of Ontario's major cities. Finally the Act has larger implications for civic life in general. It is not simply a restriction on the homeless—it functions as a set of instructions for the rest of us, teaching us how to see and respond to others in need and limiting, if not eliminating altogether, a proper place for engagement with them.

The Homeless and Social Death

The concept of social death had its origins in analyses of slave societies. Slaves were considered to have suffered a social death because they possessed three characteristics that cut them off from the rest of society. They had no money and therefore could not enter into normal exchange relations; they existed outside of enfranchised community and support systems—that is, they were natally alienated; and finally they were socially dishonoured. In her reinterpretation of social death in relation to the homeless, Liggett suggests that homeless people share this condition of social death as they exhibit all the above characteristics, and an additional fourth one—they are not needed. They are considered a surplus population, existing outside of the generative structures of society (Liggett 1991).

I have argued elsewhere that this social death is not triggered simply by the act of becoming homeless, nor are homeless people simply resigned to this condition. It must be maintained by the active patrolling of a figurative border between the homeless and other members of society, a border that reinforces the distinction between victims and agents, between those who are "homeless through incapacity" and those who are "homeless by choice." Homeless people often struggle against this social death—by being politically active, by asserting their citizenship, by organizing themselves in social groups, by developing social networks in the communities where they live, by actively creating alternative forms of living. Sometimes this has involved setting up collective campsites; organizing tents, or abandoned land along riverbeds; and in Los Angeles groups like Justiceville developed collective forms of survival, sharing tent sites and patrolling each others' meager possessions so they were safe while individuals were away at temporary work or begging (Ruddick 1991). And homeless people, contrary to theories of social disaffiliation often develop tenuous social networks by offering what skills they have—in Los Angeles this has taken the form of writing letters or translating documents for housed non-English speakers (Rowe and Wolch 1990). But in so doing, in resisting this position as victim, they risk being castigated in the media as being "mere activists" or people who cannot, *by definition* be "really homeless," or not "homeless enough" (Ruddick 1996a).

The Moral Geography of the City

For those who survive outside the market economy, it is paramount to understand both the moral and the market geography of the city. The homeless person must be able to accurately assess the "prime and marginal spaces" of the city as well as the "spatio-temporal pockets" of moral law rather than market law. Marginal spaces provide places to sleep or hang out without being evicted. Prime spaces enhance the possibilities of subsistence through begging or other activities. And the right interpretation of the moral geography of prime spaces enhances possibilities for begging or other forms of subsistence. Seventy years ago these "pockets of moral law" may have included the spaces around a church where parishioners might feel particularly generous (and pious) on a Sunday morning (Duncan 1979). Today it is more likely to be a McDonald's, where people exit with full stomachs and loose change in their pockets. The tension between these two needs—for prime and marginal space—helps to produce a peculiar geography of homeless people who often cluster in parts of the city, including particular parts of the downtown, where they have reasonable access to both.

For homeless people in general, survival also requires becoming adept at tactical appropriations of space, in and against its strategic demarcations. Tactics require the fleeting transitory use of spaces that have been strategically organized by others—those who have title to property. "A tactic," as De Certeau (1984: 36–37) notes:

is a calculated action determined by the absence of a proper locus. The space of the tactic is the space of the other ... it must play on and within a terrain imposed on it and organized by the law of foreign power ... a maneuver within the enemies' field of vision. It takes advantage of opportunities and depends on them, without any base where it could stockpile its winnings.

For homeless people tactical use of space means they often occupy spaces when they are least used or patrolled, or pretend to use these spaces for other purposes. For instance homeless people can be seen pretending to wait for the bus in order not to be accused of loitering; in Los Angeles they find places to sit or sleep in cheap movie houses; in Toronto late one winter night I observed a homeless man sleeping in the lobby of a bank that was open to allow patrons access to the automated-teller machine. The need for access to both prime and marginal space, and space that can be used for tactical purposes, helps to create a particular micro-geography of homelessness. These spatial preconditions have played out in a particular way for street kids in Toronto. They have contributed to a peculiar geography of convergence on the sidewalks of lower Yonge Street and the intersections along University Boulevard. Until recently, the seedy atmosphere of lower Yonge Street was a place where street youth could blend in and could have, should they choose, close access to services, but it is also near the Eaton Center and other stores that are filled with tourists—a continually renewable resource of potential "customers" for begging. This geography has come together, as well, for squeegee kids at various intersections along University Boulevard—not far from vacant lots and empty buildings to the east and west that have served as temporary squats, but also bottlenecked with commuters in their cars in the morning and evening rush hour.

And street youth have learned how to negotiate not simply the pockets of moral law, but pockets of market law. As observers of squeegee work have noted, many squeegee kids ran their operations like a well-tuned business. They were courteous, good humoured and knew the value of a "loss leader"—sometimes cleaning a car window for free when drivers claimed to have no cash, using a friendly smile in the hopes of building good customer relations. Press on the squeegee kids oscillated between castigating them as freeloaders "from Scarborough" and alternately celebrating their resourcefulness. More supportive newspaper accounts have depicted their activities as the creative escape from the combined effects of abuse or neglect at home, loss of government support due to cuts in assistance and limited economic opportunities with rising youth unemployment. Many accounts suggest in fact that local squeegee kids learned their trade from street youth from Quebec. In the early 1990s, the draconian turn in welfare policy for young people in Quebec, known as the "Paie" program, forced them earlier into street life than their Ontario counterparts. In Ontario, in the mid-1990s, more restrictive legislation around the reporting of abuse, which required street youth to provide evidence of abuse rather than simply assertion, contributed to the rise of kids on the streets across the province.

And the presence of street youth has been substantial. While counts of transient peoples are notoriously difficult, by 1996, service providers estimated somewhere between seven thousand and ten thousand street youth lived in Toronto, including an increased population during warm summer months (Tizzard 1997). And a large majority was escaping from situations of physical or sexual abuse or neglect (Tizzard 1997). Their tactical appropriations of city space have contributed, over the years, to the clustering of services for young people-at-risk in the downtown. Of the thirty-one services (including shelters, drop-ins and the like) serving street youth in the broader downtown, by the mid-1990s, the majority could be found along lower Yonge Street between Dundas and Bloor (see map of at risk youth services in Toronto). This pattern of convergence on particular areas of the downtown is not specific to Toronto. It has played out in many cities in North America in the formation of service-dependent ghettos for homeless people (Dear and Wolch 1987) and for street youth in particular in their gravitation to seedier, "glitz-ier" parts of the city for survival (Ruddick 1996b).

Given the ambivalent position of the media and the general public through the 1990s, the punitive reaction of the province is puzzling, the law-and-order attitude of the government aside. But the larger, strategic reorganization of the downtown reveals a different story.

Commodification of the Street and Restriction of Public Life

Over the past twenty years cities across North America have witnessed a dramatic transformation in street life. Half a century ago, in the 1950s, the street was a sign of social dysfunction reserved for the lower classes and their children, who could not afford private alternatives for leisure. "Playing in the street" and "hanging out on street corners" were subjects for study by sociologist William Whyte who in *Street Corner Society* attempted

The "At Risk" Youth Services in Toronto

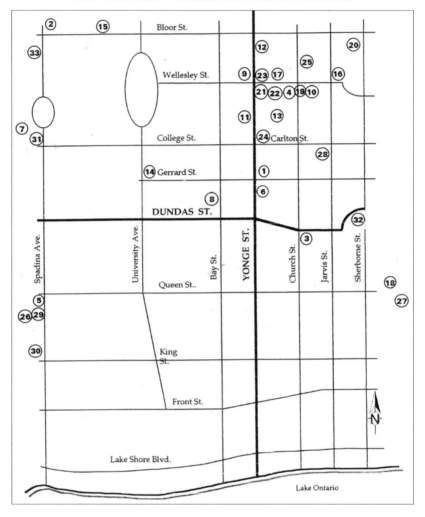

to demystify supposedly pathological behaviours of groups whose social networks were organized in and through the streets (Whyte 1943). Urban designers such as Le Corbusier, a leading figure of the modern movement in architecture and planning, vowed to "kill the street" or at least transform it into "a machine for traffic" (Gold 1998). Today, the street has come to be celebrated as a place of recreation versus pathology. Back in vogue is the "flaneur" figure from the nineteenth century—a cultured individual (usually male) who was renowned for spending his time observing street life (Wilson 1995). But this celebratory shift has not been marked by an

A.	SHELTERS	E.	COUNSELLING
1.	Covenant House	19.	YouthLink Inner City
2.	Stop 86 YMCA	20.	YouthLink Head Office
3.	Rendu House	21.	Central Toronto Youth Services
4.	Turning Point Hostel	22.	Oolagen Community Services
5.	YMCA House	23.	Lesbain Gay Community Counselling Programme
B.	DROP-INS	24.	HIV-AIDS Community Counselling Programme
6.	Evergreen Center		
7.	Drug Free Arcade	25.	519 Church Street Community Center
C.	GETTING OFF THE STREETS PROGRAMMES	F.	EMPLOYMENT TRAINING
8.	First Stop Community Information	26.	Youth Employment Services
		27.	Parachute Employment Training
9.	Street Outreach Services		
10.	Operation Go Home	G.	EDUCATION SERVICES
11.	Native Child and Family Services	28.	Beat the Street
12.	Children's Aid Society	29.	KYTES
13.	Catholic Children's Aid Society	30.	OASIS
D.	MEDICAL CLINICS	H.	FOOD AND CLOTHING
14.	Teen Clinic	31.	Scott Mission
15.	The House	32.	Street Haven
16.	SHOUT Clinic		
17.	Hassle Free Clinic	I.	LEGAL SERVICES
18.	Jessie's Center for Pregnant Teens	33.	Justice for Children

increase in open-minded public spaces. A truly open-minded public space is one that admits, allows, even encourages contradictory and conflictual uses. Berman talks about this space as providing the potential for unplanned encounters between individuals from very different walks of life. As such he imagines it potentially as a space where people can overcome biases, can express and sometimes, perhaps, even settle their differences, form new alliances, gain new insights about the potentials and possibilities of what it is to be human (Berman 1986). A truly open-minded public space represents in at its best the expansive possibilities of public space in helping to form and extend a public sphere, or in Lefebvrian terms "the right to the city" (Lefebvre 1972).

What has emerged instead is a public space that has become increasingly restricted in its uses. This has taken the form of the commodification of a kind of "safe diversity" for the middle and upper classes. White upper-

and middle-class people can sample other cultures but often as commercialized representations of the "real thing." An example is the highly patrolled space of urban and suburban malls. In addition there are increasingly strict specifications of the times when public space can be accessed and the types of activities permitted within it (Mitchell 1995; Smith 1996). This metamorphosis of the city and civic life within it is being staged through numerous projects of residential, commercial and neighbourhood revitalization, which first increase the ranks of the cities' homeless, and then evict them from the few public spaces that remain (Harvey 1989; Deutsche 1990; Smith 1996). Social life is increasingly removed from public streets and retreats to shopping malls, which restrict access to "undesirable" individuals. The residential and commercial gentrification that is part of this process reduces affordable shops and housing for low-income people. The transformation of areas like Vancouver's Gastown, Frankfurt's Alte Oper and New York's Greenwich Village are all examples of this process.

In Toronto, the downtown has experienced several, isolated transformations. These include: the growth of the condo market on the eastern side of Yonge Street; the incipient development of King-Spadina; the commercial transformation of Yonge and Dundas Streets, including the introduction of a new square, the introduction of large chain retail stores, which is crowding out the less expensive stores, and the opening of the previously self-contained Eaton Center to the western side of Yonge Street. All challenge the viability of lower-income commerce and increase pressures from invested business interests to "clean up the area." And in Toronto over the past decade, there have been numerous public and private battles about the appropriate uses of public space. The eviction of homeless people from Allen Gardens, the eviction of homeless demonstrators from Nathan Phillips Square, and the re-routing and transformation of Caribana—the local Mardi Gras—from an unbridled procession down University Boulevard to a contained, fenced-in, demarcated parade along the Lakeshore—all mark a growing restriction on the allowable uses of public spaces and the allowable publics within them.

These acts should not be read as isolated events but numerous "architectures of eviction" (Deustche 1990). And as she argues in a similar transformation of New York City:

> The effects of redevelopment in individual urban spaces are not circumscribed but radiate outward ... redevelopment projects interconnect into larger spatial patterns [and it is] possible to

discern beneath the appearance that gentrification is not a random, spontaneous act, its systemic character and far reaching proportions. (Deustche 1990: 163)

The *Safe Streets Act* must be read in the context of Deutsche's insights, as part and parcel of a series of larger transformations of public space and the public sphere. But its regulation acts more insidiously, not just on the strategic designations of prime market residential or commercial spaces—through acts of planning and development—nor on the tactical re-organization of marginal parks space, but at the level of gesture and the body. The Act moreover, does not simply regulate gestures of the homeless. It teaches the larger, potentially sympathetic public how to re-read those gestures as aggressive and alien. It transforms small acts of open-mindedness, whether in charitable giving or market exchange, into criminal complicity. The *Safe Streets Act* functions as the final stage in the metamorphosis and decimation of civic life.

References

Berman, M. 1986. "Take It to the Streets: Conflict and Community in Public Space." *Dissent* 33(4).

Dear, M. and J. Wolch. 1987. *Landscapes of Despair. From Deinstitutionalization to Homelessness*. Princeton: Princeton University Press.

De Certeau, M. 1984. *The Practice of Everyday Life*. Los Angeles: University of California Press.

Deustche, R. 1990. "Architecture of the Evicted." *Strategies: A Journal of Theory, Culture, Politics* 3.

Duncan, J. 1979. "Men without Property: The Tramps Classification and Use of Urban Space." *Antipode* 17.

Gold, J.R. 1998. "The Death of the Boulevard." In N. Fyfe (ed.), *Images of the Street*. New York: Routledge.

Harvey, D. 1989. *The Condition of Postmodernity*. Cambridge: Basil Blackwell.

Lefebvre, H. 1972. *Le Droit à la Ville*. Paris: Editions Anthropos.

Liggett, H. 1991. "Where They Don't Have to Take You In: Representations of the Homeless in Public Policy." *Journal of Planning Education and Research*. 10(3).

Mitchell, D. 1995. "The End of Public Space? People's Park, Definitions of the Public and Democracy." *Annals of the Association of American Geographers* 85(1).

Rowe, S. and J. Wolch. 1990. "Social Networks in Time and Space: Homeless Women in Skid Row, Los Angeles." *Annals of the Association of American Geographers* 80(2).

Ruddick , S. 1991. "Heterotopias of the Homeless: Strategies and Tactics of Placemaking in Los Angeles." *Strategies: A Journal of Theory, Culture, Politics* 3.

_____. 1996a "From the Politics of Homelessness to the Politics of the Homeless." In R. Keil, G.R. Wekerle, D.V.J. Bell (eds.), *Local Places in the Age of the Global City*. Montreal: Black Rose Books.

_____. 1996b. *Young and Homeless in Hollywood. Mapping Social Identities*. New York: Routledge.

Smith, N. 1996. *The New Urban Frontier: Gentrification and the Revanchist City.* New York: Routledge.

Tizzard, C. 1997. "De-Marginalizing the Marginalized: Including Street Youth in the Redevelopment of Lower Yonge Street." University of Toronto. Current Issues Paper. Programme in Planning.

Whyte, W. 1943. *Street Corner Society.* Chicago: University of Chicago Press.

Wilson, E. 1995. "The Invisible Flanuer." In S. Watson and K. Gibson (eds.), *Postmodern Cities and Spaces*. Oxford and Cambridge: Blackwell.

4.

Keeping the Streets Safe from Free Expression

Richard Moon

Introduction

When poverty activists resort to the *Canadian Charter of Rights of Freedoms*, things cannot be going very well. The *Charter of Rights* will not eliminate poverty or gross disparities in wealth. It will not ensure that affordable housing is provided to those in need. All it may be able to do is to protect the individual's right to ask others for help, to beg in the streets.

The Government of Ontario knew that a straightforward ban on begging and squeegeeing was not likely to survive constitutional challenge. And so instead of simply banning begging or squeegeeing, the *Safe Streets Act* of Ontario restricts "soliciting," which occurs when an individual "request[s], in person, the immediate provision of money or another thing of value, regardless of whether consideration is offered or provided in return, using the spoken, written or printed word, a gesture or other means." Moreover, the law does not ban all soliciting; instead it bans "aggressive" soliciting and soliciting in certain locations, such as near a bank machine, in a parking lot or on a roadway (*Safe Streets Act*, sections 1–3).

While the provincial law does not refer specifically to begging or squeegeeing, its definition of "soliciting" may not, in practice, capture much more than these activities. Because "soliciting" is limited to "in-person" requests for the "immediate provision of money" with or without "consideration" (the giving of something of value in exchange), it does not cover commercial advertising and promotion. Some exceptional forms of street vending and charitable solicitation may, in theory at least, fall within the Act's prohibition on aggressive soliciting and soliciting in particular locations. The government, however, has publicly stated that its real concern, in enacting the *Safe Streets Act*, was to get aggressive beggars and squeegee people off the streets and not to restrict ordinary charitable solicitation.

While the Act does not ban all soliciting, it does more than simply restrict aggressive soliciting/begging. Soliciting near bank machines, parking lots, pay telephones, bus stops and roadways (all prohibited by the Act) is not necessarily aggressive and is no more likely to be so than at any other public location. If the government's concern is with aggressive "soliciting," then the ban appears to be over-inclusive. Indeed, it is because the ban is over-inclusive (covering some non-aggressive soliciting) that its apparent restriction of certain forms of charitable fundraising is a source of embarrassment to the government.

The scope of the ban seems overly broad, covering certain forms of non-aggressive soliciting, including instances of charitable fundraising. However, this over-inclusion is not due to bad or careless drafting. The government's goal was to enact a ban on begging and squeegeeing that would survive constitutional review. They sought to do this by defining the banned activity so that it was in some respects broader than begging (the term soliciting is defined in an apparently content-neutral way) and in other respects narrower (aggressive soliciting or soliciting in certain locations is banned). Yet, as I will argue, the concerns that lie behind this partial ban on soliciting are the same as those that would support a general ban on begging and squeegeeing and are entirely inadequate as a basis for restricting the constitutional right to freedom of expression.

The Constitutional Right to Free Expression

A constitutional challenge to the *Safe Streets Act* may be based on several grounds. In this comment I will consider the argument that the Act violates freedom of expression, which is protected by subsection 2(b) of the *Canadian Charter of Rights and Freedoms*. I will not address the argument that the Act violates section 15 of the Charter, the right to equality. It is worth noting, however, that many of the points made in the following discussion also support the claim that section 15 of the Charter has been breached. In particular, the disadvantaged position of beggars, or of the homeless in general, is an important component of a powerful section 15 argument that the Act reflects, and further aggravates, the marginalized position of these groups.

The *Canadian Charter of Rights and Freedoms* establishes a two-step process for the adjudication of rights claims. The first step is concerned with whether a Charter right, such as freedom of expression, has been breached by a state act. The court must define the protected interest or activity (in this case, expression) and determine whether it has been interfered with by the state. At this first step, the burden of proof lies with the party claiming a breach of rights. The second step in the adjudicative process is concerned with the justification of limits on Charter rights. Section 1 of the Charter states that the protected rights and freedoms may be limited provided the limits are "prescribed by-law," "reasonable" and "demonstrably justified in a free and democratic society." The limitation decision is described by the courts as a balancing of competing interests or values. At this stage, the onus of proof lies with the party seeking to uphold the limitation, usually the state. This two-step process means that the court may find that a Charter right has been infringed, yet conclude that the infringement was reasonable and demonstrably justified and therefore not unconstitutional.

The Supreme Court of Canada has said in prior cases that the term "expression" in subsection 2(b) refers to any act that conveys a message (*Attorney General of Quebec* v. *Irwin Toy* 1989: 969). Soliciting or begging clearly fall within the protection of the right to free expression. Begging, no less than advertising or picketing, conveys a message. At minimum, begging involves a request to passers-by for money. The request may be made by spoken or written word or by holding out or displaying a cup or hat.

While the Supreme Court defines the scope of the freedom under subsection 2(b) broadly so that it protects all non-violent forms of expression, when assessing limits under section 1 of the Charter the Court distinguishes between core and marginal forms of expression, identifying different instances of expression as more or less valuable and, on that basis, as more or less vulnerable to restriction. Political expression, for example, is considered core expression because it is closely linked to the values underlying the freedom. As such it can be restricted only for the most substantial and compelling reasons. In contrast, pornography, hate speech and commercial advertising are seen as lying at the margins of the freedom's scope, because they are not so directly linked to the values underlying the freedom. The courts may be more flexible, or less demanding, in their assessment of restrictions on these forms of expression.

A key question is whether begging/soliciting should be treated either as core expression or as marginal expression; whether it should be understood as a form of political expression that lies at the core of the freedom or whether it is better understood as "commercial" in character (Hershcoff and Cohen 1991). If begging is a form of commercial expression, or at least analogous to commercial expression, then its restriction, particularly if in the form of a time, place and manner limitation or if focused on invasive or intimidating instances, may be easily justified under section 1. However, if begging is seen as political in character, restrictions will be more rigorously scrutinized and less likely to be supported under section 1 as justified limits on the constitutional right to freedom of expression.

While the courts routinely state that the category of commercial expression does not lie at the core of the freedom's protection, they say very little about why it deserves reduced protection and how it is to be distinguished from political or other forms of expression. Begging may look something like advertising, because it involves a request for money, yet the resemblance is entirely superficial. Begging involves a request for assistance and a claim of need that cannot be made to fit into the model of a commercial transaction. Regardless of whether we think begging can be described as "political" in character, it is very different from the consumer messages that dominate public discourse (discussion, conversation). Indeed, it may be that begging is experienced by some passers-by as invasive because it is so different from mainstream commercial expression. Yet it is precisely because begging takes place at the margins of public discourse that its restriction should be subject to careful examination and require substantial justification.

Marginal Expression or Expression at the Margins

Begging involves a request for money and so bears some resemblance to commercial advertising, which encourages consumers to make a product or service purchase. It is profit-oriented, using this phrase in a rather extended way. As such, the argument goes, begging is not core-value expression and so its restriction is easier to justify.

However, before making this link between begging and commercial activity or advertising, it is worth considering the basis for the courts' distinction between commercial advertising (marginal) and political (core) expression. The Supreme Court has said on many occasions that commercial expression is less valuable than other forms of expression because it is motivated by profit. However, the Court has not directly explained why this motivation is significant or how it is possible to isolate a category of profit-motivated expression in a public discourse that is dominated by commercial voices and operates on market principles.

The view that advertising does not lie at the core of the freedom and can be restricted under section 1 on less than substantial and compelling grounds is expressed at the beginning of nearly all judicial decisions concerning commercial expression. For example, in *Rocket* v. *Royal College of Dental Surgeons* (1990: 247), Madame Justice McLachlin observed that, in the case of commercial expression, the motive for imparting information is "primarily economic" and that "the loss" that censorship might cause "is merely loss of profit, and not loss of opportunity to participate in the political process or the 'marketplace of ideas', or to realize one's spirited or artistic self-fulfilment." For these reasons, said Madame Justice McLachlin, "restrictions on expression of this kind might be easier to justify than other infringements of section 2(b)" (*Rocket* v. *Royal College of Dental Surgeons* 1990: 247).

However, Madame Justice McLachlin recognized that while commercial expression may be "designed only to increase profits," it may also play "an important role in consumer choice" (*Rocket* v. *Royal College of Dental Surgeons* 1990: 247). Because the interests of the profit-motivated speaker are not significant, any value that profit-motivated (or commercial) expression may have will depend entirely on its contribution to the listener:

> These two opposing factors—that the expression is designed only to increase profit, and that the expression plays an important role in consumer choice—will be present in most if not all cases of commercial expression. Their precise mix, however, will vary greatly.... (*Rocket* v. *Royal College of Dental Surgeons* 1990: 247)

For this reason Madame Justice McLachlin thought "it is inadvisable to create a special and standardized test for restrictions on commercial speech" (*Rocket* v. *Royal College of Dental Surgeons* 1990: 247).Yet, in the later judgment of *RJR Macdonald Inc.* v. *Canada* (1995: 348), Madame Justice McLachlin argued that profit motive or economic orientation should not lessen the claim of expression to constitutional protection: "In my view, motivation to profit is irrelevant to the determination of whether the government has established that the law is reasonable or justified as an infringement of freedom of expression." She observed that profit is the motive, in whole or in part, behind a variety of expressive forms, some of which are seen as core to the freedom: "book sellers, newspaper owners, toy sellers—are all linked by their shareholder's desire to profit from the corporation's business activity, whether the expression sought to be protected is closely linked to the core values of freedom of expression or not" (*RJR Macdonald Inc.* v. *Canada (A.G.)* 1995: 348).

It is not clear whether Madame Justice McLachlin changed her mind about restrictions on commercial expression, coming to believe that commercial advertising is no less valuable than other forms of expression, or whether she simply thought that the lesser protection granted to advertising rests on something other than its profit motivation. If she was arguing the latter, and still accepted that commercial advertising lies outside the core of the freedom, she did not say what this lesser value rests on. Despite these remarks by Madame Justice McLachlin, the Supreme Court of Canada, in other judgments, such as *Hill* v. *Church of Scientology* (1995: 1174), has continued to state that "the fact that the targeted material was expression motivated by economic profit more readily justified the imposition of restrictions."

In a market economy it is difficult to isolate a category of expression for reduced protection on the basis of profit motive or commercial origin (Moon 2000: 79). Despite the Court's frequent but very general references to profit motive, two concerns seem to underlie the decision to locate commercial advertising at the margins of freedom of expression. The first has to do with the vague sense that advertising appeals are often manipulative or misleading. In *Attorney General of Quebec* v. *Irwin Toy* (1989), for example, manipulation was explicitly identified as the basis for restricting advertising directed at children.

The other concern is the power of specific advertisements, or advertising in general, to dominate discourse and displace or overwhelm other messages in the "market place" of ideas. The commercial domination of public discourse is not specifically identified as a concern in the court's commercial advertising cases, yet it may be critical to understanding the manipulative or deceptive character of particular ads and may explain the willingness of the courts to set lower standards for the restriction of advertising in general. The overwhelming number of commercial messages that we are confronted with each day means that it is simply not possible for the audience to critically reflect on the claims or associations of each. As well, the domination of public discourse by advertising means that the unnatural images or absurd associations of particular ads seem unexceptional. Finally, and most importantly, because the principal channels of public discourse are controlled by commercial interests and carry only advertising and programming funded by advertising, the underlying message of advertising, that self-realization is achieved through consumption, is an almost unchallengeable cultural assumption (Moon 2000: 81).

Yet, if these concerns, and not profit motive, underlie the reduced protection of advertising, it is not at all clear that begging should be treated as marginal expression. Begging is not simply a request for money that can be assimilated into the model of a commercial or market transaction. It is a claim of need and a request for help that falls outside the realm of commercial consumption and exchange. Only those who view all human interaction through the lens of exchange and all human value through the lens of wealth maximization or preference satisfaction could think otherwise. This barren view of human interaction is adopted by Robert Ellickson (1996: 1229), who reduces human obligation or charity to a feeling of satisfaction:

> Ordinarily, a panhandler's intended message is wholly transactional, namely, "I would like you to give me money." A beggar essentially invites a pedestrian to enter into an exchange. If the exchange were to be completed, the beggar would receive alms, and the donor would receive the feeling of satisfaction that commonly follows an act of generosity.

While many persons may sometimes feel "overwhelmed" by the large number of beggars in the downtown areas of certain cities, begging is not part of the mainstream commercial discourse. Indeed, begging is viewed as a nuisance and is experienced as invasive because it is so exceptional, because its message of need does not fit within the dominant discourse of lifestyle-based consumption.

The decision to label begging as either political or commercial seems to be governed by the decision-maker's views about social welfare. For those who see poverty and homelessness as the consequence of social-economic forces and who see current social welfare provision as inadequate, begging is a political act or an act of political expression. It is political because it reflects or manifests the deeper political/social problems of poverty and homelessness. On the other hand, for those who see poverty or homelessness as something that is within the individual's control or as something that has occurred because of choices that she/he has made (the result of personal deficiencies), begging is simply a request for money—a self-interested act that is the cause rather than the symptom of social decay. This latter view is evident in, for example, the decision of the U.S. Circuit Court in *Young* v. *New York City Transit Authority*, "the only message that we are able to espy as common to all acts of begging is that beggars want to exact money from those whom they accost … the object of begging and panhandling is the transfer of money" (*Young* v. *New York Transit Authority* 1990: 154).

Begging may not amount to a critique of the social/political order.

Nevertheless it is not simply a request for money. It is, more fundamentally, a request for help—an appeal to the audience's concern for, and sense of duty to, those in need. Behind the beggar's request is a claim of need—need for food or shelter or clothing. This claim is sometimes explicit but more often is simply implied in the request for money. It is a personal claim that can only be understood and evaluated within the social/economic context on the basis of the audience's political views.

It is to the claim of need and appeal for help that the passer-by must respond by giving money or declining to give money or apologizing for not having any change or consciously avoiding any eye contact and walking on. The passer-by may believe that the beggar does not really have such a need and is seeking to mislead her/him. Or perhaps the passer-by thinks that there is some form of need but that her/his donation will not be used appropriately, or that even if there is need, nothing is owed to the beggar, who is responsible for her/his situation. Yet regardless of whether the passer-by accepts or rejects the legitimacy of the beggar's claim/appeal, there is an engagement between strangers about need and obligation in the community. As Arthur Schafer argues (1998: 8):

> When society silences a panhandler or banishes the panhandler from places which have traditionally been public places, such banishment comes close to being a denial of recognition. Each of us has a fundamental need to be recognized by our fellow citizens as a person with needs and views. The criminalization of panhandling is not only an attack upon the income of beggars, it is an assault on their dignity and self-respect, on their right to seek self-realization through public interaction with their fellow citizens.

To deny a person the right to ask others for help seems like the most fundamental breach of freedom of expression (Schafer 1998: 10).

While begging may take place at the margins of society or at the margins of our commercially-dominated public discourse, it is not marginally connected to the values of truth, democracy and self-realization, which are said to underlie the constitutional commitment to freedom of expression (*Attorney General of Quebec* v. *Irwin Toy* 1989: 976). It may not be "political," as that term is used by democratic theorists of free speech (Meiklejohn 1965), but it is "political" in another and perhaps more profound sense of that term.

The Justification for Restricting Begging/Soliciting

The *Safe Streets Act* purports to be about aggressive or threatening soliciting or soliciting that is conducted in a persistent and harassing manner. While a commitment to freedom of expression means that an individual cannot be prevented from speaking simply because others are uncomfortable with her/his speech and find it intrusive or irritating, at a certain point expression may become so invasive or harassing that the state is justified in imposing a restriction. A ban that focuses on aggressive or persistent soliciting may be seen as protecting important individual and community interests.

The Act bans soliciting "in an aggressive manner." According to the Act, soliciting is aggressive if it is "likely to cause a reasonable person to be concerned for his or her safety or security." In addition, subsection 2(3) of the Act provides that certain listed activities "shall be deemed to be soliciting in an aggressive manner":

1. Threatening the person solicited with physical harm, by word, gesture or other means, during the solicitation or after the person solicited responds or fails to respond to the solicitation.
2. Obstructing the path of the person solicited during the solicitation or after the person solicited responds or fails to respond to the solicitation.
3. Using abusive language during the solicitation or after the person solicited responds or fails to respond to the solicitation.
4. Proceeding behind, alongside or ahead of the person solicited during the solicitation or after the person solicited fails to respond to the solicitation.
5. Soliciting while intoxicated by alcohol or drugs.
6. Continuing to solicit a person in a persistent manner after the person has responded negatively to the solicitation.

Most instances of these listed behaviours can be viewed as aggressive and as properly subject to legal restriction. However, there may be some instances that are not in fact aggressive in character; for example, the intoxicated beggar who sits out of the way with a sign or hat in front of him or her.

The Act does more than simply ban aggressive soliciting/begging. It also bans soliciting/begging in certain locations or contexts. The Act provides in subsection 3(2) that no person shall

(a) solicit a person who is using, waiting to use, or departing from an automated teller machine;
(b) solicit a person who is using or waiting to use a pay telephone or public toilet facility;
(c) solicit a person who is waiting at a taxi stand or a public transit stop;
(d) solicit a person who is in or on a public transit vehicle;
(e) solicit a person who is in the process of getting in, out of, on or off a vehicle or who is in a parking lot; or
(f) while on a roadway, solicit a person who is in or on a stopped, standing or parked vehicle.

Most anti-begging by-laws include a provision similar to this. For example, the Vancouver *By-law to Regulate and Control Panhandling*, states that "no person shall panhandle on a street within 10 metres of (a) an entrance to a bank, credit union or trust company, (b) an automated teller machine, (c) a bus stop, (d) a bus shelter, or (e) the entrance to a liquor store." However, the *Safe Streets Act*, in contrast to this and other anti-begging by-laws, does not define a particular zone (10m or otherwise) around the bank machine or bus stop in which begging is forbidden. And so under the *Safe Streets Act*, there may be some question as to when someone who has used a bank machine, for example, is still "departing" from the machine and when she/he has re-entered the general public sphere.

Begging near a parking lot or a bank machine or a bus stop may sometimes be conducted in an aggressive or harassing manner, with the beggar physically obstructing the pedestrian or verbally abusing her/him. Yet begging at these locations is not necessarily aggressive. Indeed, begging at a parking lot or a bank entrance is no more likely to be aggressive than at any other public location and may simply involve sitting with a hat or sign at one's side. The most that can be said about these regulations is that they seek to protect members of the public from communication by a beggar (aggressive or not) in situations where contact with her/him is difficult to avoid or to escape from quickly or where the "beggee" may feel more embarrassed by her/his refusal to give. The problem to which these regulations respond is not physically aggressive or intimidating or harassing begging but rather the feeling of invasion or discomfort that the passers-by may feel when confronted by, or even when confronted with, beggars.

While begging is sometimes conducted in a physically aggressive way, with the beggar obstructing or threatening the pedestrian, most begging is non-aggressive and even polite. Nevertheless, begging is experienced by many as invasive or upsetting or is labeled as aggressive even when it is not conducted in a physically threatening or persistent manner. Public reaction has become increasingly negative as begging has become more common. As Joel Blau observes: "some people are generous and do not mind occasional requests for money. Too many requests, though, soon exhaust their generosity. Losing their capacity to engage in single charitable acts, they are increasingly inclined to see homelessness as a disfigurement of the landscape, and begging as a personal assault" (Blau 1994: 137).

Yet, ironically, many people experience begging as invasive because it is not the norm, because it is so different from ordinary public interaction. They are not accustomed to being confronted by others, by strangers, and being asked for help. Indeed, many individuals seem to experience the mere presence or visibility of the homeless as invasive. They are uncomfortable with, even afraid of, those who are different from themselves and living in difficult circumstances. They see in these strangers the potential for violence. As well, they are uneasy about what the growing presence of beggars says about our community. They are not comfortable having to confront so immediately the question of their personal and shared responsibility to others.

Despite the familiar and idealized description of public/political discourse as the free and open exchange of ideas and information among citizens, the fact is that we engage in very little face-to-face communication with strangers. Most of our public discourse is mediated. It is conducted through newspapers, magazines and on television and radio. It is unidirectional, in that the vast majority of citizens receive commercial messages or commercially funded messages to which they have no real opportunity to respond. We are unaccustomed to engaging in any sort of verbal exchange with those who are not friends, family or co-workers. This is why an individual may feel invaded when she/he is addressed by strangers, by beggars. Ironically, it is the failure of mediated social provision (state-provided welfare) that has led to this increase in direct (non-mediated) contact with strangers—with the poor and the homeless.

The other factor that makes begging seem invasive is that it runs against the dominant message of public discourse. Advertising is everywhere, around every corner we turn. Yet we may not see advertising as invasive, or as invasive to the same degree as begging, precisely because it is omnipresent. Advertising defines our public discourse and shapes our assumptions about appropriate social interaction. It is a familiar part of our public environment. It is something we expect to see when we go about our day. At the same time, the domination of discourse by advertising (by consumer-oriented messages) makes begging seem invasive. The beggar's message about basic need and responsibility runs against the principal theme of commercially dominated public discourse, that personal satisfaction and fulfilment are achieved through consumption. While in some communities begging is an accepted part of public interaction, in our consumer society we have come to assume that we should be protected from uncomfortable personal interaction or from being confronted with claims of obligation.

The Supreme Court of Canada has indicated, in previous judgments, that "time, place and manner" restrictions, which are directed at the physical effects rather than the content or message of communicative activity, may be easier to justify under section 1. Because this type of restriction is aimed at the physical consequences of expression rather than at the content of the communicated message, it will often leave the individual speaker with alternative times, places and manners at/in which to communicate her/his message. The state should be permitted to introduce a reasonable restriction on the time, place and manner of expression, provided the restriction leaves adequate space for expression generally or for the expression of particular views, i.e., provided that there are other times, places and manner in which the expression can take place (*Peterborough* v. *Ramsden* 1993: 1106).

However, the *Safe Streets Act* restricts a form of communicative interaction that is linked to a particular content or message. A request "in person for the immediate provision of money or another thing of value, regardless of whether consideration is offered or provided in return" that takes place at the roadside or by a parking lot may include more than begging but not much more. It is worth noting that public streets and sidewalks may be the only places available for a beggar to communicate her/his message. Merchandisers and charitable fundraisers will often have other options. And while the law might in fact restrict some forms of charitable solicitation, such as selling chocolate bars beside a parking lot, it is difficult to imagine that the police would ever enforce the law in this situation. These charitable organizations are seen as doing good work and as causing no obvious harm. Yet this assumption about who will and will not be prosecuted is a reminder of the law's real purpose—the removal of beggars and squeegee people from the streets.

A good example of the selective enforcement of the Act involves an organization in Windsor known as the Goodfellows. This organization has for many years provided Christmas food and gift hampers to poorer families in the city. The Goodfellows raise money over the Christmas period by selling their "newspaper" at the major road intersections in the city. They (enthusiastically) approach cars stopped at traffic lights and ask for a "donation" in exchange for the paper. I describe this as a donation because the newspaper is only two pages in length and simply describes the Goodfellows' charitable project. The driver, who makes a donation, then places the Goodfellows' newspaper on her/his dashboard so that it is visible. By doing this she/he avoids any further approaches and requests. The fundraising activities of the Windsor Goodfellows is almost certainly prohibited by the *Safe Streets Act*. However, the Windsor police have agreed to allow the Goodfellows to fundraise at road intersections provided they do not act in an aggressive or dangerous manner.

In addition, while the Act does not restrict soliciting/begging in general, and appears to leave some space for lawful begging, it does not restrict soliciting/begging simply on the basis of its harmful physical consequences. The law prohibits soliciting/begging that is neither persistent nor aggressive. The content or message of the communication is a critical part of what the law seeks to curtail. Begging is banned or restricted because it is experienced by passers-by as invasive, and it is experienced in this way because of its message. Because the law restricts a particular kind of communication and because it does so for reasons that relate, at least in part, to who the speaker is and what she or he is saying, it cannot truly be described as "time, place and manner" or "content-neutral" in form and so must be subject to a rigorous standard of review under section 1 of the Charter. It is difficult to see how this restriction on requests for aid by some of the most marginalized members of the community could meet this standard.

References

Attorney-General of Quebec v. *Irwin Toy*. 1989. *Supreme Court Reports* 1.

Blau, J. 1994. In R. Fantasia and M. Isserman (eds.), *Homelessness: A Sourcebook*. New York: Facts on File Inc.

Ellickson, R. 1996. "Controlling Chronic Misconduct in City Spaces: Of Panhandlers, Skid Rows, and Public-Space Zoning." *Yale Law Journal* 105.

Hershcoff, H., and A.S. Cohen. 1991. "Begging to Differ: The First Amendment and the Right to Beg." *Harvard Law Review* 104.

Hill v. *Church of Scientology of Toronto*. 1995. *Supreme Court Reports* 2.

Meiklejohn, A. 1965. *Political Freedom*. New York: Oxford University Press.

Moon, R. 2000. *The Constitutional Protection of Freedom of Expression*. Toronto: University of Toronto Press.

Peterborough v. *Ramsden*. 1993. *Supreme Court Reports* 2.

RJR Macdonald Inc. v. *Canada (Attorney General)*. 1995. *Supreme Court Reports* 3.

Rocket v. *Royal College of Dental Surgeons*. 1990. *Supreme Court Reports* 2.

Safe Streets Act, 1999, S.O. 1999, c.8

Schafer A. 1998. "Down and Out in Winnipeg and Toronto: The Ethics of Legislating Against Panhandling." Online: Caledon Institute of Public Policy Homepage— http://www.caledonist.org/full91.htm.

Young v. *New York Transit Authority*. 1990. *Federal Reporter* 2d series 903.

5.

The Constitutional Disorder of the Safe Streets Act:
A Federalism Analysis

David Schneiderman

Introduction

In contemporary western societies, citizenship is constructed now more than ever around the values of the market. Freedom is on offer to those who choose to participate in the multiple market exchanges that proliferate in everyday life. Consumerism—the ability to consume goods and services from any place and to travel anywhere—offers a space of freedom to those who face obstacles in most other areas of their lives (Hall 1996: 234). Political actors understand the significance of this conception of citizenship. More often than not, they choose to trade social welfare for greater purchasing power by reducing taxes and the size of public expenditure (Williams 1961: 325). There are, of course, those who wish to resist this form of political life, and so they unplug their cable, join in consumer boycotts or engage in acts of protest or civil disobedience at Seattle or Quebec City.

Then there are those who are denied this semblance of agency, those who have no capacity to participate in modern consumerism because they are poor, without work or homeless. They are designated "failed" (Rose 1998: 79) or "flawed" consumers (Bauman 1998: 38) and "inadequate" (Bauman 1998: 38) or "anti-" (Rose 1998: 79) citizens. These individuals are hard to understand, for they are deemed to have chosen this form of lifestyle. Having voluntarily removed themselves from the civil order they constitute a problem of disorder. Analysis accordingly shifts from the causes of poverty—jobless growth and sustained unemployment—to "the behaviour of the poor as the problem" (Procacci 1998: 23). Poverty thereby becomes a problem to be regulated by criminal prohibition.

In *Madness and Civilization*, Michel Foucault describes the "great confinement" and forced labour of the poor in seventeenth-century Europe as animated by moral disapproval. In the European mind, the poor "cross[ed] the frontiers of bourgeois order of his [or her] own accord; and alienate[d] himself [or herself] outside the sacred limits of its ethic" (Foucault 1965: 58). The strategic response today is to seek the ethical rehabilitation of the poor or, alternatively, to banish them from sight. Those who refuse to govern themselves as productive citizens "have also refused the offer to become members of our moral community," writes Nikolas Rose. For them, it seems, "harsh measures are entirely appropriate" (Rose 1999: 267).

The Ontario *Safe Streets Act* exhibits this sort of moral disapproval. The purported intention of this provincial Act is to remove from public sight individuals whose conduct is deemed to have crossed the frontier of our social and ethical order: the beggars, the squeegee kids and the homeless, those who have "voluntarily" removed themselves from our moral community. If the impetus of the law is to express disapproval of conduct that crosses the frontier of moral order, this makes the law constitutionally suspect. It may be that this subject matter belongs more appropriately to the federal government as a matter for the criminal law. If so, the *Safe Streets Act* is beyond the authority of the provincial government.

The federal government alone has authority to make the criminal law of Canada. The provinces, in contrast, are allocated responsibility for the administration of justice in the province—in effect, they enforce the federal criminal law. Provinces also have authority to attach penalties to provincial offences, that is, offences of provincial laws validly authorized under one of the classes of subjects listed in section 92 of the *Constitution Act, 1982*. For our purposes, provinces have authority to make laws that concern the regulation of streets, sidewalks and highways and the suppression of conditions likely to give rise to the commission of crimes.

This essay's inquiry into the scope of provincial authority suggests that the provincial government may have overstepped its authority in regard to the "solicitation" provisions of the Act—those provisions concerning aggressive begging or begging of a so-called "captive" audience. This essay does not address other aspects of the Act, such as amendments to the *Highway Traffic Act* that prohibit squeegeeing or prohibitions on the disposal of condoms or needles in public spaces. However one characterizes these latter provisions, as concerning the regulation of a specific trade, regulations concerning road safety or removing conditions ancillary to crime, they are more impervious to the charge of usurping the federal criminal law power than are the provisions regarding aggressive begging.

Federalism analysis is not ordinarily concerned with the moral rightness of legislation. I would maintain, however, that federalism analysis often is a value-driven exercise, represented by past choices and present-day evaluations of social problems. Admittedly, this sort of analysis has nothing to do with solving the root problems that give rise to the problem of poverty in Canada. Federalism analysis offers only a formalistic and formulaic response to what are complex social problems. But this remains a fruitful enterprise, as the division of power analysis helps to uncover the moral impetus for the legislation and its connections to techniques of governance related to neo-liberalism and economic globalization. The ultimate judicial resolution of this constitutional question also may reveal the degree to which these governance techniques have affected other branches of the state. It may disclose whether there is a judicial propensity to banish the poor from judicial concern while at the same time tightening the hold of consumer citizenship in Canadian constitutional law.[1]

The Federal Criminal Law Power

According to post-World War II Canadian judicial interpretation, there is virtually nothing beyond the purview of the federal criminal law power. In an era of increasing devolution, untied funding and withdrawal of state regulation over matters concerning the economy, the criminal law power remains one of the few legitimate levers of control available to the national government. This, I would claim, is no mere coincidence. Economic globalization constructs a realm beyond the reach of ordinary politics. There are few things left for states to do other than to secure the conditions for the smooth operation of the market and related concerns regarding personal safety and security. This helps to explain the politics of vengeance that dominates provincial and national politics. What governments *can do* is legislate in regard to safety, the "only field," Zygmunt Bauman (1999: 5) writes, "in which something can be done and seen to be done." It is the desire of the government of Ontario to enter into this field that helps to explain the impetus for the Act.

The federal criminal law power long has had a centralizing influence on Canadian public policy. The authority of the federal government to make criminal law is traceable back to the conquest of the French in North America. Several years later, the *Quebec Act, 1774* restored the civil law and preserved Roman Catholic religious education and institutions but provided no exemption from application of the English criminal law. The unifying feature of the criminal law was not lost on the framers of the 1867 *British North America Act* (Friedland 1984: 49).

Though its definition has been an elusive one, the judiciary traditionally has granted the federal criminal law power a wide ambit, and this continues to the present day. Most recently, in the *Gun Control Reference*, the Supreme Court of Canada reaffirmed the capacity of the federal government to make criminal law in a wide range of areas using a variety of legislative mechanisms (*Reference Re Firearms Act* 2000). This capacity is subject to the formal requirement that criminal law is that which is framed as a prohibition with a penalty and which has a "criminal public purpose." The latter was famously defined by Justice Ivan Rand in the *Margarine Reference* as having to do with "public peace, order, security, health, [and] morality." These were the "ordinary though not exclusive ends served" by the criminal law (*Reference re Validity of Section 5(1) of the Dairy Industry Act* 1949: 49).

The test of criminal public purpose addresses the question of "colourability" (*RJR Macdonald Inc.* v. *Canada (Attorney General)* 1995: para. 122)—the disguised attempt to invade the other's jurisdictional field. But valid criminal public purposes have included restrictions on tobacco advertising in order to promote health (*RJR Macdonald Inc.* v. *Canada (Attorney General)* 1995) and regulatory mechanisms for the identification of prohibited toxic substances under the Canadian *Environmental Protection Act* (*R.* v. *Hydro-Quebec* 1997). The purpose of the criminal law, wrote Justice LaForest, is to "underline and protect our fundamental values" (*R.* v. *Hydro-Quebec* 1997: para. 127), and the criminal law power must keep pace with those changing values.[2] Thus, "it is entirely within the discretion of Parliament to determine what evil it wishes by penal prohibition to suppress and what threatened interest it thereby wishes to safeguard" (*R.* v. *Hydro-Quebec* 1997: para.119). The real force of the criminal law power arises in those instances where provincial laws are challenged for intruding into the federal field (Hutchinson and Schneiderman 1995: 16)—when provincial laws are tested for their colourability.

Provincial Powers
The modern law of Canadian federalism analysis, however, grants a wide ambit for both federal and provincial legislative authority, in this field as in others. Courts have upheld provincial laws that regulate a variety of forms of conduct covered by the federal *Criminal Code*, so long as they are validly enacted for provincial purposes. In the *Rio Hotel* case, for instance, New Brunswick could attach as a condition to liquor licensing a ban on nude

performances of the sort prohibited by the "public nudity" provisions of the *Criminal Code* (*Rio Hotel Ltd.* v. *New Brunswick* 1987). In the infamous *Dupond* case, a Montreal municipal by-law prohibited assemblies, parades or other gatherings where there were reasonable grounds to believe that they would endanger safety, peace or public order (a temporary ordinance also prohibited any assembly, parade or gathering for a thirty-day period). The Supreme Court of Canada upheld the municipal actions, characterizing them as preventive, not punitive measures, intended to prevent "conditions conducive to breaches of the peace and detrimental to the administration of justice" (*Attorney General Canada* v. *Dupond* 1978: 435). The measures concerned unlawful activities—namely unlawful assemblies and riots—but before they had yet taken place and so were "complementary" to federal legislation.

The law of Canadian federalism condones concurrency. So long as the prohibition relates to a valid provincial purpose, provincial law may cover the same field as the federal criminal law. Should there be conflict, the provincial will yield to the federal to the extent of the inconsistency. On occasion, though, the Supreme Court of Canada has been less tolerant of provincial incursions into the criminal law field. The rationales for these decisions may have something to do with the fact that they concern traditional criminal subject areas like prostitution and abortion. The focus for the Court in these cases again is colourability—a veiled attempt to invade the other's jurisdiction in the guise of valid provincial law. The Court undertakes this task by looking beyond form, or "beyond the four corners of the legislation" (*R.* v. *Morgentaler* 1993: 497). Two cases of this sort form a backdrop to the current analysis.

The *Westendorp* case concerned a Calgary municipal by-law purportedly to deal with prostitutes gathering on the street and, according to the by-law's recitals, attracting crowds, creating "annoyance and embarrassment" and impeding the "right and ability" of the public "to move freely and peacefully on the streets" (*Westendorp* v. *The Queen* 1983: 49). The purported object of the by-law concerned movement on municipal property—its streets and sidewalks—a matter legitimately within the authority of municipalities as delegates of the provincial government. The Supreme Court looked beyond the recitals, however. The by-law prohibited not the blocking of passageways but soliciting for the purposes of prostitution, precisely the type of conduct prohibited by the old soliciting provisions of the *Criminal Code*.

The 1993 *Morgentaler* case is even more instructive. In the wake of the Supreme Court of Canada's decision declaring invalid the *Criminal Code* prohibitions concerning access to therapeutic abortions (*R. v. Morgentaler* 1988), the Nova Scotia Legislative Assembly prohibited the performance of abortions outside of hospitals. The *Medical Services Act* was enacted and its regulations promulgated, solely in response to Dr. Henry Morgentaler's establishment of a free-standing abortion clinic in Nova Scotia. The stated intention of the enactment was to "prohibit the privatization of the provision of certain medical services in order to maintain a single high-quality health-care delivery system for all Nova Scotians" (*R. v. Morgentaler* 1988: 470). This stated purpose certainly was within the purview of the province, but the Supreme Court of Canada, in a unanimous judgement, looked beyond "the four corners" of the Act: to Morgentaler's opening of a clinic as providing the impetus for the legislature to act; to the legislative debates, which disclosed little or no concern for privatization or quality control; to the lack of any study on cost control or consultation with the medical profession; and to the severity of the penalties (fines ranged from $10,000 to $50,000). The primary object of the legislation, the Court concluded, was to prohibit "socially undesirable conduct … from the viewpoint of public wrongs or crimes" (*R. v. Morgentaler* 1988: 513).

A similar analysis can be undertaken in regard to the Ontario *Safe Streets Act*. Bearing in mind that modern law of Canadian federalism grants a wide berth to legislatures to attach penalties to validly enacted laws concerning economic regulation and social policy, what does the text of the Act, and the circumstances giving rise to it, tell us about its dominant purpose?

The Disorder of the Law

The Ontario Tories in their 1999 election campaign "Blueprint" outlined a commitment to outlaw "behaviour that jeopardizes the safe use of the streets" (Ontario *Legislative Debates,* November 2, 1999). The *Safe Streets Act* was meant to fulfil that promise. The Act outlaws not only squeegee people on Ontario roads but solicitation in an "aggressive manner … likely to cause a reasonable person to be concerned for his or her safety or security." Certain activities are "deemed to be" aggressive solicitation, including threatening persons by word or gesture in the course of solicitation, obstructing a person's path, using abusive language, proceeding behind, alongside or ahead of a person, soliciting while intoxicated, or continuing to solicit after being refused. In addition, solicitation of a so-called "captive audience" is prohibited, including solicitation of persons at teller ma-chines, pay telephones or toilets, waiting at a transit stop or getting in or out of vehicles. Persons found guilty of these offences can be fined up to five hundred dollars on a first conviction and up to one thousand dollars or six months imprisonment on each subsequent conviction.

Note that the solicitation provisions of the Act are only secondarily concerned with the movement of persons on streets and sidewalks (a matter within provincial legislative competence). Many of the activities considered to be aggressive solicitation, such as using abusive language or soliciting while intoxicated, are only remotely connected to securing safe passage for pedestrians on sidewalks and streets. Similarly, begging outside of pay telephones, bus stops or banking machines bears only a remote relationship to impeding movement. None of these are very well anchored in provincial authority. Only two examples of deemed aggressive soliciting directly concern impeding a person's progress, and these are "obstructing a person's path" or proceeding "behind, alongside, or ahead of a person." The dominant purpose revealed by the Act as a whole has more to do with regulating behaviour found to be offensive by some (what the Tory "Blue-print" called "threatening and harassing behaviour") than the regulation of streets and sidewalks. Moreover, the fines seem high given the nature of the offence, and this is particularly so for repeat offenders. The Act also entitles police officers to arrest without warrant those persons who are reasonably believed to have offended the Act in order to establish their identity. Given the purported objective of the legislation, to regulate the safe use of streets and public spaces, arrest without warrant seems either like legislative overreaction or intrusion into the criminal law field.

An important consideration is the fact that the provincial offences defined in the Act bear strong similarity to a number of existing *Criminal Code* offences. In this way, the Act appears to do more than merely prevent the conditions giving rise to crime. General Counsel of the Canadian Civil Liberties Association, Alan Borovoy, underlined this point in testimony to the Ontario Standing Committee on Justice and Social Policy. Where the Act "does address issues of harm," he declared, it is "probably already unlawful" (Ontario Standing Committee on Justice and Social Policy 1999). *Criminal Code* offences like "intimidation" (section 423[1]), "har-assment" (section 264) "uttering threats" (section 264), "threatened as-sault" (section 265), "extortion" (section 346), and "common nuisance" (section 180) effectively cover the same territory. The *Safe Streets Act* not only replicates existing *Criminal Code* offences, it reinstitutes the offence of vagrancy, which was removed from the *Criminal Code* in 1972. The old vagrancy provisions made it an offence to beg from door to door in a public place and to "wander or trespass without means of support."[3]

What do the legislative debates disclose? When he introduced Bill 8 (the *Safe Streets Act*) in the Ontario Legislature, Jim Flaherty, Attorney General for Ontario, confirmed that the purpose of the Bill was to guarantee the people of Ontario the right to be in public spaces in a "safe and secure manner," "without being or feeling intimidated." "They must be able to carry out their daily activities without fear," he declared. The Bill responded to these concerns by regulating conduct "that interferes with the safe use of public spaces" (Ontario Legislature, November 2, 1999). The Minister nevertheless stressed the language of movement and safety, subjects more appropriately within provincial purview.[4] Speaking on behalf of the Government on third reading of the bill, Gerry Martinuk (MLA for Cambridge) maintained that Bill 8 was "designed to regulate the use of our sidewalks, streets and other public places" (Ontario Legislature, November 7, 1999). Martinuk also explained that the Bill was about controlling "disorder." Drawing on the Tories' "broken window" strategy, he stated that if "there is disorder on our streets, people will vacate our streets out of concern for their safety and that void will be filled by additional crime" (Ontario Legislature, November 7, 1999).

The discourse of "disorder" also was employed by Staff Sergeant Ken Kinsman of the Toronto Police Service. In his testimony concerning Bill 8 before the Ontario Standing Committee on Justice and Social Policy, Staff Sergeant Kinsmen invoked the image of a "pyramid of crime." "Astride the top of the pyramid were street-level drug dealers, and at the bottom were "graffiti and garbage issues." Somewhere near the bottom was the category of disorderly behaviour, which lumped together "publicly intoxicated, aggressive panhandlers" and squeegee people. Kinsmen maintained that "disorder issues are the most serious problem facing communities today" (Ontario Standing Committee on Justice and Social Policy 1999).

Other circumstances surrounding the passage of the Bill also suggest legislation in the nature of the federal criminal law rather than mere provincial regulation of street safety. There appeared to be no research data documenting the incidence of aggressive begging or the panhandling of captive audiences.[5] In her testimony before the Justice and Social Policy Committee, Laurie Rector, Executive Director of the National Anti-Poverty Organization, submitted that "to date there is no substantive evidence that points to the fact that panhandlers or squeegee people pose a danger to anyone" (Ontario Standing Committee on Justice and Social Policy 1999). Lastly, the legislation was rushed into passage both before the Committee and in the Ontario Legislative Assembly. Liberal MLA Michael Bryant claimed that the law was "rammed through, fast-tracked and no attention was paid to the [drafting of the] bill whatsoever" (Ontario Legislature, December 7, 1999).

Much of this suggests that the *Safe Streets Act* is in the nature of the "prohibition of socially undesirable conduct," to borrow a phrase from Justice Sopinka in *Morgentaler*. Yet there is one further set of reasons having to do with the moral nature of the legislation that signals its status as criminal law.

The Morality of Disorder

With no apparent empirical evidence to justify the vague and broad prohibitions on "aggressive begging" and soliciting a "captive audience," the impetus for the Act might be traceable to the pressures generated by "agents of moral reform" (Hunt 1999: 214). Admittedly, the general anxieties associated with the rise of economic globalization and the spread of neo-liberalism alone are insufficient to explain "either the timing or the specific configuration of a moral reform campaign" (Hunt 1999: 214). If approached with some caution, however, drawing linkages to the fears and anxieties associated with the presence of poor people in the midst of plenty may be instructive when it comes to characterizing the dominant purpose of the legislation.

The Act, in brief, gives expression to the discomfort many feel when confronted directly by the poor. Recall that the definition of aggressive solicitation turns not on the conduct of the solicitor but on the feeling of safety and security of the person being solicited (the provision reads: "likely to cause a reasonable person to be concerned for his or her safety or security.") Herbert Gans writes that "the feelings harboured by the more fortunate classes about the poor [are a] mixture of fear, anger and disapproval, but fear may be the most important element in the mixture" (Gans 1995: 75). This fear is generated, in part, by the impression that street beggars have chosen voluntarily to live outside of "civil society": the society constituted by the consumer lifestyle that the publics of the North Atlantic economies have embraced so enthusiastically. The poor seemingly have refused to live by "the bonds of civility and responsibility" (Rose 1999: 259); they have elected to spurn consumer citizenship. The associated anxieties resemble the nineteenth-century discourses concerning "pauperism" (Dean 1991: 174) and "the residuum" typically characterized as the "economically dead" (Cruikshank 1999: 15). According to Barbara Cruikshank, what placed the poor "outside society as a whole" was the perception "not that they had the wrong values but that they had no values" (Cruikshank 1999: 15).

Disapproval of this lifestyle choice "is topped up by fear; non-obedience to the work ethic becomes a *fearful* act, in addition to being morally odious and repulsive" (Bauman 1998: 77). Having refused to become ethically responsible citizens, harsh measures seem appropriate. Neo-liberal forms of governance require the management of groups according to their dangerousness (Rose 1999: 236), and so begging is classified as a dangerous act, endangering the safety and security of civil society. No attempts at rehabilitation are made; the underclass of beggars and panhandlers are beyond reprieve. The reduction of their visible presence is the only manageable option.

These are the ends served by the *Safe Streets Act*, its self-proclaimed dominant purpose: to improve feelings of safety and security of those who fear the poor, hungry and indigent. Just as it is the role of the state to improve conditions for the smooth operation of the market, so it is its role to improve feelings of safety and security of those who participate in the market: politics intervenes to "create the organizational and subjective conditions for entrepreneurship" (Rose 1999: 144).

That the *Safe Streets Act* links up neatly to neo-Foucauldian work on "moral regulation" hardly qualifies it as criminal law. But this analysis should help to situate the Act in a larger discourse about security and threats to freedom based on behaviour that is deemed to have "crossed the frontier of ... social order" (Foucault 1965: 58). It is this kind of expression of "fundamental values," to borrow a phrase from Justice LaForest, that more appropriately belongs in the realm of the criminal law.

At the same time as we characterize the legislation as moralistic and criminal in nature, we are confronted with the same "inevitable compromises" as those seeking to challenge the authority of the provinces to regulate access to abortion (Gavigan and Jenson 1992: 144). By claiming that a large part of the *Safe Streets Act* can only validly be enacted by the federal Parliament, we should not be seen to be endorsing the criminalization of conduct better regulated by provincial health and welfare legislation. Indeed, the conduct at issue is more appropriately the subject of laws securing the satisfaction of basic human needs—health and welfare measures concerning minimum-income and minimum-wage laws—and not the exercise of the criminal law power. In this way, constitutional analysis based on the division of legislative powers leads to a different kind of risk, a constitutional disorder of another sort.

Notes

1. I have addressed the judicial role in valourizing consumer freedom elsewhere. See Schneiderman 1998.
2. Jean Leclair writes that this enlarged scope for the criminal law power enables courts to contribute to the construction of a national identity (Leclair 1998: 376).
3. See the original offences in the *Criminal Code,* 55 & 56 Vict., c.29, ss.207–09 and the last version in S.C. 1954–55, c.51, Ss.160, 164, 182 and 372. The provisions were repealed in S.C.1972, c. 13, s.12. I am grateful to Joe Hermer for his genealogy of begging as a crime of vagrancy.
4. Motorists were blocked by squeegee people and shoppers by aggressive solicitation.
5. Frank Mazzilli (MLA for London-Fanshawe) explained that "people" told the government that they have been threatened with physical harm, that they have had their path obstructed during and after being solicited, that they have been subjected to abusive language, followed, approached by people under the influence of alcohol or drugs, and solicited even after they had said no (Ontario Standing Committee on Justice and Social Policy 1999).

References

Attorney General of Canada v. *Dupond.* 1978. *Supreme Court Reports* 2.

Bauman, Z. 1999. *In Search of Politics.* Stanford: Stanford University Press.

_____. 1998. *Work, Consumerism and the New Poor.* Buckingham: Open University Press.

Cruikshank, B. 1999. *The Will to Empower: Democratic Citizens and Other Subjects.* Ithaca: Cornell University Press.

Dean, M. 1991. *The Constitution of Poverty: Toward a Genealogy of Liberal Governance.* London: Routledge.

Foucault, M. 1965. *Madness and Civilization: A History of Insanity in the Age of Reason.* Translation Richard Howard. New York: Vintage Books.

Friedland, M.L. 1984. "Criminal Justice and the Constitutional Division of Power in Canada." In Friedland (ed.), *A Century of Criminal Justice: Perspectives on the Development of Canadian Law.* Toronto: Caswell.

Gans, Herbert. 1995. *The War Against the Poor.* New York: Basic Books.

Gavigan, S., and Jane Jenson. 1992. "Beyond Morgentaler: The Legal Regulation of Reproduction." In J. Brodie, S. Gavigan and J. Jenson (eds.), *The Politics of Abortion.* Toronto: Oxford University Press.

Hall, S. 1996. "The Meaning of New Times." In David Morley and Kuan-Hsing Chen (eds.), *Stuart Hall: Critical Dialogues in Cultural Studies.* London: Routledge.

Hunt. A. 1999. *Governing Morals: A History of Moral Regulation.* Cambridge:

Cambridge University Press.

Hutchinson, A.C., and David Schneiderman. 1995. "Smoking Guns: The Federal Government Confronts the Tobacco and Gun Lobbies." *Constitutional Forum* 7.

Leclair, J. 1998. "The Supreme Court, the Environment, and the Construction of National Identity." *Review of Constitutional Studies* 4, 372.

Ontario Legislature. 1999. *Legislative Debates.* November 2, November 7 and December 7.

Ontario Standing Committee on Justice and Social Policy. 1999. 1st Sess., 37th Parl. Nov. 29.

Procacci, G. 1998. "Poor Citizens: Social Citizenship and the Crisis of Welfare States." In S. Hanninen (ed.), *Displacement of Social Policies.* Jyvasklya: Social Philosophy.

Reference re Firearms Act. 2000. Supreme Court Reports 1.

Reference re Validity of Section 5(1) of the Dairy Industry Act. 1949. Supreme Court Reports.

R. v. Hydro-Quebec. 1997. Supreme Court Reports 3.

R. v. Morgentaler. 1988. Supreme Court Reports 1.

R. v. Morgentaler. 1993. Supreme Court Reports 1.

Rio Hotel Ltd. v. New Brunswick (Liquor Licensing Board). 1987. Supreme Court Reports 2.

RJR Macdonald Inc v. Canada (Attorney General). 1995. Supreme Court Reports 3.

Rose, N. 1999. *Powers of Freedom: Reforming Political Thought.* Cambridge: Cambridge University Press.

_____. 1998. "The Crisis of the Social: Beyond the Social Question." In Sakari Hanninen (ed.), *Displacement of Social Policies.* Jyvasklya: Social Philosophy.

Safe Streets Act, 1999, S.O. 1999, c.8

Schneiderman, D. 1998. "Constitutionalizing the Culture—Ideology of Consumerism." *Social and Legal Studies* 7 (2).

Westendorp v. The Queen. 1983. Supreme Court Reports 1.

Williams, R. 1961. *The Long Revolution.* Harmondsworth: Penguin.

6.

Demonizing Youth, Marketing Fear:
The New Politics of Crime

Dianne Martin

Introduction

Crime rates are dropping, the economy is booming and Canada is once again, according to the United Nations, one of the "best countries" in the world (United Nations 2000). Yet fear of crime is a crippling, "top of mind" concern, and the new millennium is witnessing the sharpest distinction between the living conditions of the rich and poor since the Great Depression. Paradox or conundrum, this reality is shaping criminal justice in Canada, and it is a fearful, rather mean reality, dominated by an ethos that blames poverty on the poor and assumes that a life of privilege is the right of those fortunate enough to be born to it. It is represented in so-called law-and-order political campaigns, demands for harsher punishment, bigger prisons, for no parole and no mercy. It is perhaps most starkly represented in quasi-criminal legislation enacted by provinces to punish and control the adults and youth driven to the streets to sleep under bridges and to beg in the streets (to borrow from Anatole France). The paradox is sharp. In a time and in a nation of plenty, thousands of adults, children and youth live on the streets and are reduced to begging, marginal efforts at work and petty crime. Hundreds of thousands more live in shelters or are a step away from shelters. The response of legislators to the failure of current policies to provide food and shelter for all is punishment and prison for the poor. Thus we now have legislation designed to imprison the children driven to prostitution and the adults and youth reduced to begging, squeegeeing and sleeping rough. What is going on? Why has a harsh approach to crime and disorder become a central feature of our culture?

It is helpful to remember that the criminal law has always served many purposes and has always been used to advance the interests of the state. In British history, for example, the king's promise to guarantee security, safety and prompt retribution for victims of crime replaced kin-based vengeance and feud and was essential to establishing central government, the rule of law and a modern state. That promise remains fundamental to continued state legitimacy today. Political interests of all stripes are carefully attentive to issues of criminal justice as they seek to ensure continued consent and compliance with their agendas.

It is relatively easy to politicize crime because crime, and more importantly fear of crime, is part of the culture. Crime is an endlessly fascinating commodity for writers, artists, the media and all who rely on shaping popular culture for their own ends. Because of that fascination and emotional power, the architects of privatization and government restructuring have quite naturally intensified what this chapter refers to as the commodification of crime as a way to popularize their policies. That means that the ways by which crime is defined, prosecuted and punished have been influenced by ever more overtly political ends. This chapter considers this phenomenon in the context of the current treatment of street youth by examining changes to the institutions of social welfare and social justice and arguing that "crime" itself has become a commodity of political significance.

The "New" Welfare State

The so-called new welfare state draws equally from neo-conservative and neo-liberal values and is a particularly harsh place for children and youth. On the one hand, neo-conservatives argue that the family (and the church) should be the source of charity and support for the unfortunate. They view state entitlements such as welfare as an assault on these institutions and have worked hard to cut back sharply on any social assistance granted as a right, particularly to children, youth and single mothers. On the other hand, neo-liberals argue for a sort of survival-of-the-fittest reliance on market forces. The state should get out of the way of the forces that decide which regions, and which people, prosper and which don't. The only assistance the state should provide are "incentives" to work. The result of the marriage of these two views in conservative governments across Canada, but most markedly in Alberta and Ontario, is a dramatic shrinking of the social safety net. Harsh welfare cuts (a 21.6% cut in rates in Ontario for example) and strict new rules limiting entitlement popularized by the rhetoric of neo-conservatism were introduced with little warning and no provisions to allow people who were already living on very little to adjust to such a dramatic drop in their incomes. Rents have been deregulated and social housing programs dropped. These decisions have contributed to an increase in homelessness and visible poverty in all parts of the country but most dramatically in the cities.[1] In turn, this new presence of homeless and disenfranchised young adults on the street, in full view of respectable citizens, has reinforced the arguments of neo-liberals that these social failures must be made "responsible" for themselves or face the consequences (Fraser 1993: 9; Gordon et al. 1988: 609). The effect of these policies has been exceptionally hard on youth.

There have always been reasons why some children and youth have been forced, or have chosen, to leave home, ranging from serious abuse and deprivation to less dramatic cases of not getting along. We have long made provisions, although never entirely satisfactory, for these young people. Young children who cannot live with their biological families are made wards of the state. While older children and youth (fourteen and older) who left their homes have had fewer options, until the harsh reforms of the mid-1990s they were at least eligible for a form of social assistance known as "student welfare," that is, if these youths remained in school, they received social assistance to cover rent and food. That assistance is effectively no longer available to youth who cannot live at home. Student welfare was constructed as an affront to the prerogatives and the responsibilities of families. Social conservatives argued successfully that the availability of social assistance (inappropriately) *encouraged* kids to leave home and thus won its virtual elimination. The result is that most of the youth who leave home today have very few options available for the basics of survival—food, clothing and shelter. Not surprisingly a significant number turn to—or are captured by—street prostitution (Department of Justice 1998). The rest juggle part-time minimum wage jobs, panhandle, wash windshields, engage in crime—or starve. For some, the reasons to leave home are so serious that life on, or nearly on the street, with all its dangers and degradation, is an improvement. For others, whose reasons do not stand up to comparison with life on the street, the route home is much longer if drugs, prostitution or crime have intervened.

Cuts to children's aid society budgets have removed another strand in the safety net that used to be available to catch some kids some of the time. Although children who were made wards of the state before their fourteenth birthday may still be eligible for support and assistance until they reach twenty-one, there is almost no protection in the child welfare system for older youth. Very little is available for those who enter care when they are over fourteen, even if the reasons involve abuse or sexual exploitation, and those over sixteen are, for all intents, considered "adults" with almost no claim to protection under child welfare legislation. However, changes in approach and attitude are every bit as important as these legislative limits. Most of the resources of staff, time and money that children's aid societies have available in a time of shrinking budgets, expanding case loads and a loss of legitimacy are directed to very young children (Alberta's Opposition 1997; OACAS 1993–1998; Robin 1999; Brian 1997; Welsh and Donovan 1997).

The education system is also being "reformed." Students with special needs will find fewer teachers who specialize in working with them and significantly reduced resources for the programs that help. Alternative schools and alternative programs are being cut, and adult education as a fail-safe is also becoming a thing of the past for those who cannot afford private tuition. School funding formulas are changing so that the drop-out kid is a liability to school boards, who only receive funding based on the students who remain enrolled for a full year. Touted as an important means to hold schools and teachers accountable for the success of their students, this change in funding has too often ensured the death of flexible, part-time programs that have been keeping some kids at least tenuously attached to the education system. Once again the street becomes the only option. When these funding changes are coupled with current policies around a "zero tolerance" to school violence (which ensure that students engaged in almost any sort of violence may be expelled), we have literally guaranteed that certain young people have nowhere to go but the street, and at the same time they are demonized and marginalized by the education system. If their school problems are aggravated by difficult or fragile connections to a family home, young people expelled from school under zero tolerance policies very rapidly run out of options—except for property crime, prostitution, drugs or all three (Blouin and Martino 1986: 81; Murphy and Cool 1990).

The totality of these policies is that the least fortunate among a generation of youth receive little or no support from the social welfare regime, from child welfare authorities or from the school system. Left to their own devices, usually on the street, they are also demonized as dangerous and lawless and bear the brunt of campaigns that have politicized criminal justice in unprecedented ways.

The Commodification of Crime

Crime has become a valuable political commodity. Crime-control strategies have always operated to serve privilege, control dissent and construct paradigms to explain social dysfunction, because the fear of crime has always had less to do with the incidence of crime than with justifying increasing disparity in income and well-being between classes and people (Hay 1975; 1992). As that disparity has widened, concern about crime has become a feature in literally all political campaigns today, even in the face of significant declines in the rate of crime (Carey 2000; Roberts and Doob 1990). Crime has always been a commodity to some extent, of course, if only as a means to "sell newspapers." Lurid, sensational, titillating and terrifying crime stories touch something in us; and crime (and its punishment) has long been capitalized upon to teach, to entertain and to manipulate (Hay 1975). The techniques and strategies utilized for these purposes inevitably reflect and serve their own times (appearing quaint and obvious to later times), and not surprisingly, in this period of privatization, resurgence of the market economy and relentless commercialization, crime (and its control) is literally being marketed, like any other product or service, by both the private and the public sectors. To appreciate the marketing power of crime one need only reflect on the remarkably successful campaign that persuaded millions of women and those who loved them that a cell phone for the car was essential to their safety in a country where crime against the occupants of motor vehicles is almost non-existent.

Crime is no longer simply something with marketing power, however. Crime itself, or more accurately, the fear of crime, is being marketed for political purpose. A demand from voters for more safety, more control, more order and more punishment is fostered. Middle-class markets are targeted as new laws are developed and new fears are identified—and each time, a political benefit is extracted. For example, in the 1998 provincial election in Ontario, an aggressive and punitive approach to young offenders was identified by a political pollster as, "a good issue for the 'PCs' to trot out as an election issue because it tends to appeal more to the PC voters.... Everybody likes a tough stance on crime.... If the PCs want to make it an issue and say, 'Look, the place has gone to hell in a hand basket,' they could possibly do that" (Rusk 1998).

Every aspect of the criminal process has been affected by commodification and privatization, from the definition of crime to its punishment. Common perceptions about "crime" are shaped so that "crime" is limited to street crime and disorder and to random acts of extreme violence. It would not do to recognize that corporate, or so-called "white collar," deviance causes considerably more social harm than street crime ever can (Pearce and Snider 1992). A subset of this construction contributes to the belief that the criminal justice system is "broken," that crime is "out of control," that criminals are "getting away with murder." This construction assists political agendas because it contributes to, and reinforces, an exaggerated fear of crime, irrespective of actual rates of victimization (Keane 1995). Fear of crime and lack of faith in existing institutions serves a particular political agenda because these emotionally charged fears divert attention away from more complex and politically volatile and concretely based issues, such as concern about the environment, homelessness or inequality. This fear, whether spurious, exaggerated or materially based—or not—in turn legitimates politically expedient promises of get-tough, law-and-order "solutions" that pose little threat to entrenched interests. The corollary is that perceptions about social well-being and security are also shaped, with the result that harsh "reforms" to the processes of criminal sanctions are perceived and experienced as both necessary and effective—the only possible solution to middle-class anxiety.

At the same time, and to the same end, divisions between us are reinforced and legitimated. Women, youth and minorities are dehumanized, demonized and eroticized. Gender, race and class are established in many ways, and the practices by which crime is defined and managed by police represent some of the most effective. Class, economic status and social location generally play a pivotal role in whether or not police, the system's gatekeepers, ever observe and police a particular individual—and once brought in to the criminal justice system, few escape. Conduct that is widespread across class and social location, such as truancy, use of soft drugs, various acts of "disorder," is primarily criminalized among those who are being intensively policed (Cole et al. 1995). Race and gender operate as further highly discriminatory filters (Martin 1998; Cole et al. 1995).

In addition to the targeting of marginalized adults and youth, the commodification strategy reveals how gendered the criminal justice system is. Significant money and resources from both corporate and state sources are made available to strategies and campaigns that reinforce women's role as crime *victims*. Of course, only some crimes against some women receive this support (Martin 1998; Martin and Mosher 1995; Valverde 1991: 44; Walkowitz 1992: 81). "Good" women and "innocent" children (the pairing and the depiction are deliberate) are represented as the ultimate beneficiaries of the protection and safety that the criminal justice system promises. At the same time women as good citizens and good mothers participate as frequent, if not always willing, partners in many criminal law "reforms" that strengthen the coercive power of the state. There is often little option. The prosecution process may be selective and politicized, but crimes of domestic and sexual violence are real and devastating. The criminal justice system is a significant resource and often the only resource that can be readily accessed. Thus women, as crime victims, are posed in opposition to the men who are cast as crime perpetrators. This position, however, means that women are silenced as allies to those constructed as criminal—poor, young, minority men—and are hampered in the struggle to dismantle the oppressive power relations that impact on all who are marginalized in this society; women, youth and minorities are key examples. Women in conflict with the law, on the other hand, are invisible in public and political discussion. The female accused of a criminal offence is an aberration. She is politically impotent at the same time that she is turned into either an object of scorn or a feature of erotic fantasy (Adelberg and Currie 1987; Faith 1993).

The use of the criminal sanction expands in this way because privatization does not always involve restrictions on state action. When the criminal sanction is invoked to support restructuring, both the scope and the reach of retributive influences increase. Under a neo-liberal fiscal agenda, for example, private security, policing and correctional services expand, and treatment and social services are privatized, while public institutions face cuts and private charities remain the preferred means to deliver services to offenders and victims. On the other hand, in aid of a neo-conservative moral agenda, a law-and-order retributive approach to social disorder and dysfunction is offered to reinforce hierarchical/patriarchal social organization. The former claims to celebrate the autonomous individual and thus argues for the elimination of all but the most essential intrusions by the state onto freedom of choice and action, while the latter insists on a combination of punishment and the charitable "rescue-and-reform" model for the few social services that survive. However, even when advanced as a way to cut costs and to restore governance to individuals, these policies have only selectively curtailed the reach of the state. When put into practice, privatizing interventions have been restricted to decisions to close half-way houses, to shut down beds in treatment centres and to significantly cut the budgets of agencies such as children's aid societies, leaving the retributive agencies—courts and police—in place (Ismael and Vaillancourt 1988; Mays 1995: 41; Wright 1993: 1). At the same time, neo-conservative ideology places a Christian heterosexual bourgeois family at the centre of its worldview and thus promotes a fairly aggressive legislative role in restoring this family to its proper place in the social order. In aid of this vision, state expenditure on crime has, in fact, *increased* under restructuring, with crime commissions, more police, more prosecutors and more prisons, while private enterprise provides "strict treatment facilities" and "boot camps" (Martin 1998).

Of course the two approaches, neo-conservative and neo-liberal, are not particularly inconsistent if criminal law is recognized as fundamental to the preservation and reinforcement of existing power relations. The combined effect of cuts and new initiatives reduces the state's ameliorative role while expanding its coercive power. These steps are justified as returning us to an idealized past when the streets were safe, families were intact and demands on the state were humble and modest. The real purpose of course, conscious or not, is to strengthen the reach of the criminal justice system and extend its scope against selected targets. The criminal law, after all, represents the ultimate intrusion of the state into the lives of its citizens, and when enlisted in the service of a right-wing restructuring, can be expected to do what it has always done—to control the "dangerous classes" (Silver 1992) and to advance the interests of the money classes and the new economy (Pearce and Snider 1992). The introduction of an organized police force in Victorian Britain was justified on the grounds that the poor displaced from farms and villages and attracted to (or forced to) urban factory work would be effectively controlled by a full-time police service—who would never disturb the privacy and interests of the governing classes (Silver 1992). That mandate has persisted. On one hand, the law's reach against corporate deviance (from environmental crimes to economic misconduct) is diminished in scope and impact while investigative and prosecutorial infrastructures are dismantled in the name of "cutting red tape" and "getting government out of the boardrooms of the nation" (Cavaluzzo 2000). On the other hand, street youth, beggars and "squeegee kids" are increasingly demonized and criminalized. Ontario's *Safe Streets Act* and Alberta's *Protection of Children Involved in Prostitution Act* are two of the clearest examples of the latter.

Although aggressively marketed as innovative and tough responses to the failures of existing criminal law processes, these statutes are actually redundant exercises of quasi-criminal legislation enacted with overtly political goals in mind—clearly marketed to serve political, not legislative, interests. In other words, they are usually not needed if existing legislation were actually used. They exist not to solve real problems but as political commodities. For example, this kind of legislation is increasingly *brand-named*—the work of marketers, not that of legislators or of policy makers. In the United States, Megan's Laws (sex-offender notification laws) are being passed in state after state. In Ontario we have a Christopher's Law to create a registry of known sex offenders and a Brian's Law to force mentally ill persons into treatment (Mallan 2000). These laws are identified with a victim's name—in effect a brand-name—and not by content. Victims and their survivors are encouraged to find significance for their terrible loss in this way, gaining tangible evidence that their loss was not in vain in that they have taken a step to ensure that no one else will need to suffer as they have. That more often than not the promise is at best speculative and at worst utterly empty is at the moment of little significance. In fact, the failure of many of these reforms is itself a form of planned obsolescence, effective for fuelling new harsher measures.

A similar strategy names a piece of legislation with its message. The *Safe Streets Act* is a good example. It is designed to criminalize begging and street life, but it promises an anodyne—safe streets. It is self-descriptive: "An Act to promote safety in Ontario by prohibiting aggressive solicitation, solicitation of persons in certain places and disposal of dangerous things in certain places and to amend the *Highway Traffic Act* to regulate certain activities on roadways" (*Safe Streets Act* 1999). The *Protection of Children Involved in Prostitution Act,* aimed at the coerced removal of young prostitutes from the street, in effect in Alberta and proposed in Ontario, is similar. Once again, there is instant identification, at an emotional level, with the issue. Debate or critique is almost impossible with this technique. Who wants unsafe streets? Who would refuse to protect children? Who wishes to re-victimize Brian and family or Christopher and his?

In an early and influential study of a highly politicized use of, and response to, a social issue, Stanley Cohen identified the cycle of a "moral panic" and evocatively characterized the exaggerated and distorted response to groups of youth known as "mods and rockers" in 1960s Britain. In a period of rapid and disruptive social change (not so different from current conditions) youth gangs known as "mods" and "rockers" were popularly and hysterically linked to an exaggerated rash of street crime such as mugging. With little or no evidence to substantiate the connection, draconian laws against youth were instantly demanded and enacted (Cohen 1972). In a similar vein, feminists have traced the ways that multi-faceted struggles for gender equality and freedom from the violence of wife assault, for example, were narrowed into campaigns that simply produced an enhanced criminal law strategy. The state "hears" only what it wants to hear. Complex social issues are narrowed and reframed into the language and discourse of victim and victimizer, crime and punishment. For example, the complex social and economic issues implicated in wife assault and the equally complex solutions advanced by the women's movement to serve the interests of a wide range of victims and offenders have all been subsumed into a single criminalization strategy that many women are avoiding and resisting (Currie 1990; Martin and Mosher 1995; Snider 1990; Walker 1990). Political parties and institutions appropriated the issues and the discourse concerning familial violence in a way that served partisan political as well as state interests. The result has been that women seeking equality and freedom from intimate violence are made accomplices to a range of criminalization strategies (Daly 1994; Martin 1998).

Current responses to street youth demonstrate this pattern in the context of intensive privatization. The laws primarily dealing with street youth (the *Safe Streets Act* and the *Protection of Children Involved in Prostitution Act*) have the elements of a moral panic similar to the one Cohen described (exaggeration of the phenomenon and an exaggerated response to it for example). The moral panic phenomenon is marked by a spontaneous, exaggerated, unfounded but sincere reaction by the media, the public and the legislature to an issue that inspires almost instant fear and panic. The reaction to the fact and presence of homeless youth is a much more deliberately structured pro-active strategy by government than the moral panic model connotes. Rather, elements of a moral panic have been adopted and appropriated (with much else) to the service of multiple interests—a sign of the new politics of crime. The current "crisis" about street youth as a threat and a menace requiring government action is expressed in a marketing campaign, selling fear along with a solution—crime control. The technique requires that real and complex issues concerning youth are obfuscated and obscured, while the solutions offered do not claim any new resources.

Conclusion

Laws like the *Safe Streets Act* are not designed to actually address real problems; they are drafted, brand-named and marketed to serve a political goal. The novel and sudden presence of more homeless adults and youth on Canada's city streets than have been present since the Great Depression is fairly obviously the result of economic forces and factors. However, laws like the *Safe Streets Act* work to try to ensure that this phenomenon will not be seen as a matter of economic or social justice. Rather, homelessness and poverty are articulated as a decline in moral values and an increase in disorder. Indeed there is little more to the Act than its lengthy title—and nothing of substance is done to make streets safer. Rather, the *sight* of poverty is criminalized. "Aggressive" begging is outlawed—passive, invisible begging is not. Begging in any location where the solicitation is hard to ignore, near automated bank machines for example, is criminalized while begging where the beggar can be ignored is not. And squeegeeing— the hallmark of street-youth poverty and resilience—is banned entirely. None of these provisions were needed in any real sense. The police have ample powers and plenty of crimes to choose from in the *Criminal Code* to curtail harassment, loitering and nuisance. This legislation was needed only to demonize the growing underclass and to exhibit political will.

The same can be said of Alberta's evocatively entitled *Protection of Children Involved in Prostitution Act*. It is a punitive law, permitting arrest and detention, designed to remove from city streets the unsettling sight of very young women working as prostitutes. Child welfare laws and child welfare workers are in place in Alberta (and in every province) to protect children, but these statutes and these agencies were not utilized to "protect" youthful prostitutes. Instead, the *police* were "empowered" to arrest and detain them. In Alberta where the law was enacted, and in Ontario where it is contemplated, the tragic and sordid stories of individual girls are told and retold and offered as incontrovertible "proof" that a crisis exists. Male youth are more frequently demonized as a threatening presence; their squeegees described as weapons, their appearance derided. However the so-called solutions provided for both—punitive coercive mechanisms with social welfare overtones for the child (read, "girl") prostitutes, and harsh anti-begging laws for the others—answer the needs of both crime fighters and victim saviours.

This use of crime as a political commodity serving very real right-wing political interests explains why in a time of falling crime rates and an expanding economy, a law-and-order agenda dominates public policy. Crime sells because it salves the conscience of the middle classes, transforming decisions to send children to private schools, to move to gated communities and to pay for health care privately from a matter of elite privilege to one of justified concern for family. When government cannot meet the impossibly elevated standards of security and safety they have promoted as they cut the institutions that actually do reduce crime, the demonization of criminals serves the same agenda. It becomes "common sense" first to resent "high" taxes, "wasteful" social services and "ineffective" law and order institutions, and then to support changing them by further cutting social services while making law and order institutions "more effective" (read, "punitive"). Infinitely elastic, always available, crime is the ultimate post-modern political product.

Note

1. It is helpful to remember that until the 1990s Canadian cities had very few homeless people, in sharp contrast to American cities for example, and street begging was rare.

References

Adelberg, Ellen, and Claudia Currie (eds.). 1987. *Too Few to Count: Canadian Women in Conflict with the Law.* Vancouver: Press Gang Publishers.

Alberta's Official Opposition. 1997. *To Fend For Themselves: Alberta's Approach to Reforming Child Welfare.* Report released by MLA Linda Sloan, June 25.

Blouin, J., and M.J. Martino. 1986. "Drop Out." *L'Actualitie* 11.

Brian, L. 1997. "Alberta's Abused Children Wait-listed for Aid." *Globe and Mail,* October 17.

Carey, E. 2000. "Stats Show Crime is Down—So Why Don't We Believe Them? Reality Check. The Majority of Canadians Think that Crime is Increasing, When in Reality, It's Going Down." *Toronto Star*, July 23.

Cavaluzzo, Jean Smith. 2000. "Ontario's System of Two-tiered Justice." *Toronto Star,* August 7.

Cohen, S. 1972. *Folk Devils and Moral Panics.* London: MacGibbon and Kee Ltd.

Cole, D.P., M. Tan, M. Gittens, T. Williams, E. Ratushwy, and S.S. Rajah, Commissioners. 1995. *Report of the Commission on Systemic Racism in the Ontario Criminal Justice System.* Toronto: Queen's Printer for Ontario.

Currie, D.H. 1990. "Battered Women and the State: From the Failure of Theory to a Theory of Failure." *Journal of Human Justice* 1(2).

Daly, K. 1994. "Men's Violence, Victim Advocacy and Feminist Redress." *Law and Society* 28.

Department of Justice. 1998. Federal/Provincial/Territorial Working Group on Prostitution. *Report and Recommendations in Respect of Legislation, Policy and Practices Concerning Prostitution-Related Activities.* Ottawa: Department of Justice.

Faith, K. 1993. *Unruly Women: The Politics of Confinement and Resistance.* Vancouver: Press Gang Publishers.

Fraser, N. 1993. "Clintonism, Welfare and the Antisocial Wage: The Emergence of a Neoliberal Political Imaginary." *Rethinking Marxism* 6(1).

Gordon, L., et al. 1988. "What does Welfare Regulate?" *Social Research* 55(4).

Hay, D. 1975. "Property, Authority and the Criminal Law." In Douglas Hay et al. (eds.), *Albion's Fatal Tree: Crime and Society in Eighteenth-Century England.*

New York: Pantheon Books.

_____. 1992. "Time, Inequality, and Law's Violence." In Austin Sarat and Thomas R. Kearns (eds.), *Law's Violence*. Ann Arbor: University of Michigan Press.

Ismael, J.S., and Y. Vaillancourt (eds.). 1988. *Privatization and Provincial Social Services in Canada: Policy, Administration and Service Delivery*. Edmonton: University of Alberta Press.

Keane, C. 1995. "Victimization and fear: Assessing the role of offender and offence." *Canadian Journal of Criminology* 37(3).

Mallan, C. 2000. "'Brian's Law' Passes Hurdle. Health Act Changes Could Force Treatment for Mentally Ill." *Toronto Star*, June 8.

Martin, D.L. 1998. "Retribution Revisited: A Reconsideration of Feminist Criminal Law Reform Strategies." *Osgoode Hall Law Journal* 36.

Martin, D.L., and J. Mosher. 1995. "Unkept Promises: Experiences of Immigrant Women with the Neo-criminalization of Wife Assault." *Canadian Journal of Women and Law* 8.

Mays, S.L. 1995. "Privatization of Municipal Services: A Contagion in the Body Politic." *Duquesne Law Review* 34.

Murphy, H.C., and J. Cool. 1990. "Dropping Out and Dropping In." *A Study of Youth and Literacy*. Ottawa: The Canadian Youth Foundation.

Ontario Association of Children's Aid Societies (OACAS). 1993–1998. "ACAS Fact Sheets." 75 Front Street East, Suite 203, Toronto, Ontario, M5E 1V9. Interview, Diane Cresswell, Manager of Communications. July 9, 1999.

Pearce, F., and L. Snider. 1992. "Crimes of the Powerful: Contemporary Approaches to Corporate Crime." *Journal of Human Justice* 3(2).

Roberts, J.V., and A.N. Doob. 1990. "News Media Influences on Public Views of Sentencing." *Law & Human Behaviour* 14.

Robin, H. 1999. "Program to Stop Runaways Chopped. Children's Aid Blames Provincial Changes in Welfare Funding." *Toronto Star*, April 8.

Rusk, James. 1998. "Tory panel wants to crack down on Ontario's youthcrime. Tough position may be sound election strategy, pollster says." *Globe and Mail*, June2,

Safe Streets Act, 1999, S.O. 1999, c.8

Silver, A. 1992. "The Demand for Order in Civil Society: A Review of Some Themes in the History of Urban Crime, Police and Riot." In K. McCormick and L. Visano (eds.), *Understanding Policing*. Toronto: Canadian Scholars Press.

Snider, L. 1990. "The Potential of the Criminal Justice System to Promote Feminist Concerns." *Studies in Law, Politics and Society* 10.

United Nations Human Development Report. 2000.

Valverde, M. 1991. *The Age of Light, Soap and Water: Moral Reform in English Canada, 1885–1920*. Toronto: McClelland and Stewart.

Walker, G. 1990. *Family Violence and the Women's Movement: The Conceptual Politics of Struggle*. Toronto: University of Toronto Press.

Walkowitz, J.R. 1992. *City of Dreadful Delight: Narratives of Sexual Danger in Late Victorian London.* Chicago: The University of Chicago Press.

Welsh, M., and K. Donovan. 1997. "We Need Cash and Workers Not Studies, CAS Staff Say." *Toronto Star*, August 22.

Wright, M. 1993. "A Critique of the Public Choice Theory Case for Privatization: Rhetoric and Reality." *Ottawa Law Review* 25(1).

7.

Correctional Renewal Without the Frills:
The Politics of "Get Tough" Punishment in Ontario

Dawn Moore and Kelly Hannah-Moffat

We will never build glorified country clubs to house Ontario's inmates. We have, instead, instituted a tough no frills correctional institution that sends the message that crime does not pay.
—Ontario Minister of Corrections Rob Sampson (OMCS 2000)

Introduction

The neo-conservative government of Ontario has initiated wide ranging reforms in programs of social welfare and criminal justice. From the policing of the Ontario *Safe Streets Act* against visibly indigent people to new ways of regulating social welfare recipients, a key aspect of the "common sense" revolution has been a new appetite for penalty and punishment. Indeed, the particular brand of moralizing politics generated by this neo-conservative project has very much relied on a gallery of disorderly figures that can be singled out for public ridicule and shame. Single mothers on welfare, squeegee kids and "aggressive" beggars are three of the most frequently evoked figures in an attempt to portray a climate of disorder that must be re-policed by "get-tough" policies. Nowhere can this shift to a more punitive mode be seen than in the character of correctional reforms. Along with talk about correctional "renewal," Ontario's newly revived Ministry of Correctional Services has devised a plan for corrections that invokes two of the most salient mantras of the new right: "cutting costs" while "getting tough on criminals." Most significantly, the government has called a halt to decarceration practices established in the 1980s, favouring a nostalgic notion of corrections that pines for a harsher, albeit mythical, era. This move to a punitive-based penal agenda is reaffirmed and justified through an emotional denunciation of the "club fed" approach of federal correctional policy. Golf courses, riding stables and eat-in kitchens, automatic release of violent offenders and aggressive reintegration policies are embellished depictions of federal punishment. Alternatively, the Ontario Correctional Renewal Project (OCRP) envisions privatized correctional facilities and newly constructed "super jails" that rely heavily on static electronic surveillance, minimal staffing and a marked reduction in parole releases. Ill-defined and vague notions of safety, security, efficiency and effectiveness are the essential components of this get-tough custodial initiative. These underlying narratives are consistently juxtaposed to federal liberal penal policies, which are portrayed by Ontario Tory politicians as "soft on crime" and insensitive to victims' rights.

This chapter outlines some of the recent shifts in Ontario penal governance in the context of this new climate of disorder. First, we analyze the re-definition of punishment from notions of rehabilitation and reintegration, which were linked to a pre-conservative era of decarceration politics, to a renewed emphasis on retribution and deterrence that are aligned with market-economy politics. Second, we examine how this reform has moved towards "get-tough" efficiency and away from community-based alternatives to incarceration and offender reintegration. This shift in correctional reform is accompanied by a disturbing silence around gender and ethno-cultural issues. Third, we argue that the Ontario government's OCRP initiative reflects what Jonathan Simon (1995: 32) calls "a willful nostalgia," wherein images of a disappearing virtuous and mythical past are invoked to render inevitable the need for particular social reform initiatives. While Simon (1995: 30–31) notes legal reforms are often vehicles for "nostalgia," these reform strategies that evoke a willful nostalgia often distort the past and thrive on its improbability, falseness and artificiality. In its extreme form the emergent politics of punishment in Ontario reflects renewed aspects of retribution and "cruelty."[1] In many instances, OCRP resurrects and repackages previously abandoned or de-legitimized approaches to offender management while claiming to make corrections more accountable and efficient. The renewed emphasis on deterrence and public protection implies that the "corrections of the past" achieved the objectives of deterrence, reduced recidivism and so-called safe streets.

Ontario's Reformist Penal Past
While it is difficult to decipher the gaps between political rhetoric and day-to-day operations (and we can only hope there is one), it is clear that an ideological shift has occurred in Ontario correctional policy. The

current punitive, militaristic, get-tough/no-frills sensibilities reflected in Ontario's correctional talk differs significantly from the post-WWII reformist approach to correctional policy. Since the mid-1960s, Ontario corrections focused on the ideal of rehabilitation, staff training, offender reintegration and increased community involvement in corrections, both in terms of volunteerism and in expanding the use of community-based agencies (McMahon 1992: 88). From 1960 to the mid-1970s, Ontario correctional initiatives stressed rehabilitative initiatives such as the expansion of treatment programs and the hiring of psychologists, psychiatrists and professionally trained social workers. Parole was seen as integral to the rehabilitative process and to the eventual and inevitable reintegration of the offender into the community. In the 1970s, the provincial minister of Correctional Services, Alan Grossman, openly advocated for rehabilitative policies, while denouncing past dehumanizing correctional practices. For instance, Grossman was reportedly enraged when he learned about an incident where an inmate in one institution had been strapped to a chair so that his hair could be cut short. He argued that such acts were unjustifiable practices that simply destroyed the prisoner's self-esteem (Oliver 1992: 178). Such abuses of power were considered counterproductive to the advancement of rehabilitative objectives. The correctional rhetoric of the day stressed an "Ontario Plan" that outlined elaborate descriptions of new buildings (prisons) and therapeutic communities designed in a manner conducive to rehabilitation, new staff training models and a commitment to an expanding range of therapeutic, recreational, educational and social services designed to address the needs of offenders (McMahon 1992; Oliver 1992; Winterdyk 2000). The Mimico, Monteith and Ontario correctional centres all implemented "cutting edge" treatment programs for substance abusers and sex offenders, the first-ever programs in any Canadian prison to address the specific needs of these populations. These prisons offered intensive treatment environments, with the Ontario Correctional Institute (OCI) in particular earning the reputation of being a world leader in offender rehabilitation. One of the primary goals of corrections became offender rehabilitation, which sought to prevent future criminality through the creation of "good citizens."

The increased emphasis on community-based corrections and offender reintegration meant the government invested more heavily in community initiatives than in prisons. Nevertheless, while less emphasis was placed on rehabilitation in Ontario prisons from the 1980s onwards, provincial correctional institutions continued to offer a wide range of programs and individual treatment services.

Ontario correctional policies in the late 1980s also began to identify the importance of gender and racial discrimination. In the early 1990s, the Women's Issues Task Force was established by the Ministry of Correctional Services to formulate long-term policy recommendations for women in the provincial correctional system and to develop an implementation plan that included specific actions and timelines to address the long-term policy initiatives. Similar to federal correctional officials who had recently accepted the recommendations of the 1990 Task Force on Federally Sentenced Women, the Ontario Women's Issues Task Force acknowledged that female offenders had distinct needs that were different from their male counterparts and thus required different interventions and different correctional environments. Like the federal task force, the women's issues task force involved a partnership between correctional and ministry staff, community agencies, like the Elizabeth Fry Society, and others. Their 1995 report, *Women's Voices, Women's Choices,* identified the need for correctional policy to "acknowledge that wider systemic barriers such as poverty, unemployment, lack of education, racism and sexism are related to women's involvement with the law and to their rehabilitation" (WITF 1993: 6). They set out a vision for correctional reform that mirrored the recommendations of the 1990 Task Force on Federally Sentenced Women. This task force argued that incarceration options for women should be a last resort and that existing institutions and programs for women should be modified to reflect three guiding principles: first, that the reform of the current system of female corrections in Ontario be supported by the removal of systemic barriers and include the promotion of shared responsibility for the provision of services; second, that the principles of respect, dignity and empowerment become the basis of all policy and programs so that women are enabled to make responsible and meaningful choices; and third, that women be provided with holistic healing and culturally sensitive environments that acknowledge their needs and life experiences in the context of their involvement with the criminal justice system. These principles and their related objectives set an ideal vision of women-centred correctional reform that was less repressive than that of the federal government's but nevertheless placed a considerable emphasis on holistic, gendered and culturally sensitive correctional programming.

The social and political importance of culturally appropriate programming was further underscored by the 1995 Report of the Commission on Systemic Racism in the Ontario Criminal Justice System. The Commission's investigation into Ontario prisons revealed evidence of racial hostility and intolerance in prison environments, the practice of racial segregation of prisons within and among prisons and racial inequality in the delivery of prison services (CSROCJS 1995: ii). The Commission made a series of recommendations that they believed would eliminate some of the observable forms of overt and systemic racism apparent in Ontario correctional settings.

This emphasis on rehabilitation and reintegrative community correctional approaches was also typical of federal correctional initiatives. Although the ideal of rehabilitation was tempered in the late 1970s as a consequence of extensive criticisms from across the political spectrum, Canadian correctional officials continued to support the basic premise of rehabilitation. Federal correctional researchers and bureaucrats, for example, argue that implementing, administering and evaluating offender treatment programs is a central component of contemporary "corrections" (Gendreau et al. 2000). A vast amount of human and fiscal resources are currently devoted to identifying and implementing "what works" in terms of federal correctional programming.

"Get-tough" Efficiency

In Ontario the correctional pendulum has swung. The so-called new conservative correctional rhetoric of the late 1990s no longer stressed the importance of community corrections, gender or cultural sensitivity and the role of socio-structural factors (like poverty) in the decisions of offenders. There is little evidence of a reasoned or informed correctional strategy based on a careful analysis of past mistakes and best practices in correctional planning. Current rhetoric tacitly rejects rehabilitative approaches to crime and instead favours an *inexpensive, harsh, militaristic, deterrence-based accountability model*. The law-and-order politics promoted in Ontario is comparable to that of many American jurisdictions. It draws on a common set of themes, which include expressivity, punitiveness, victim-centredness, public protection, exclusion, enhanced control and public/private partnerships. And this new emphasis calls for more punitive penal strategies including harsh sentencing, increased use of prisons, "truth in sentencing" and parole-release restrictions, austere prisons, boot camps, "supermax" prisons (highly secure specialized handling units), the revival of chain gangs, community notification laws and zero-tolerance policies (Garland 2001: 369). This perspective and its related strategies presume the political support of citizens who are seen as fearful of crime and as intolerant of "soft" governmental approaches to crime control, themselves partly responsible for the "crime problem." Garland (2001: 350) argues that resurgences of:

harsh punishments and the forceful rhetoric of "law and order" are deployed by the state as a commanding gesture of lordship and popular reassurance, and find support in the general public, for whom this process of condemnation and punishment serve as an expressive release of tension and a gratifying moment of unity in the face of crime.

This expressive element of penality has a long and complex relationship to penal policy.

Rather than the postwar image of the prison *as* punishment, current government rhetoric promotes the idea that prison is a place *to be* punished and punishment for its own sake. It promotes a "penality of cruelty" (Simon 2001: 127), which is a trend towards "penalties that are painful, vengeful, and destructive of the penitent in body as well as life chances." The justification for such punishments goes beyond the belief in the necessity of harsh penalties for the purpose of crime control or even to satisfy an abstract notion of retribution. A disturbing and prominent feature of this "penality of cruelty" is a "satisfaction at the suffering implied by, or imposed by, punishments upon criminals, as well as emotions of anger and desire for vengeance taking violence" (Simon 2001: 126). The reform and reintegration of offenders into the community through the use of parole, for example, are firmly rejected. It is suggested that aggressive early release strategies compromise "public safety" and that parole is a *privilege* that must be earned. The correctional agenda, previously constructed as concerned with humane, gendered and rehabilitative effectiveness, is now focused on fiscal accountability and questions of efficiency. This type of rhetoric holds great purchase in a market economy and is particularly useful in Ontario, where initiatives to toughen-up the criminal justice system are attractively packaged. This punitive-efficient correctional rhetoric is populist and politicized, meaning that "policy measures are constructed in ways that privilege public opinion over the views of criminal justice experts," (Garland 2001: 350–51). Not surprisingly many of the initiatives promoted under the get-tough mantra and that result from the withdrawing of the so-called frills of social services are under researched and lack the elaborate costing schemes and statistical projections that are standardized features of much social policy (Garland 2001: 350–51).

International correctional research clearly shows that threatening and coercive approaches to crime control or offenders rarely, if ever, affect recidivism. Regimentation, austerity and deprivation have been used repeatedly in penal practices throughout history and have repeatedly been shown to fail. The principle of lesser eligibility[2] formed the basis of some of the western world's earliest carceral systems (Spirenburg 1984). When these attempts were shown as failures in reducing recidivism, they were replaced by military-style practices such as head shaving and regimented movements such as marching. These too were quickly revealed as ineffective and counterproductive to the projects of deterrence and reform.

While there is a dearth of research on similar practices carried out today, the studies that do exist on more (or less) modernized versions of the same fundamental practices display similar results. Current studies suggest that boot camps and shock-incarceration programs are in fact more likely to nurture criminality and deviance among prisoners than they are to reform them (MacKenzie et al. 1995; Petrosino et al. 2000). Likewise, supermax[3] prisons, incorporating shock-incarceration-style practices with the promise of efficiency and greater public safety, have proved ineffective on all counts. The use of supermaxes in the United States has been causally linked to the expansion of the U.S. penal industry, indicating a subsequent increase in government spending where decreases were promised. Amassing such large numbers of offenders also gives rise to security concerns. Perhaps the most salient example of these security concerns is the privately run supermax in Youngstown, Ohio, which was plagued with disasters during the first year it was open, including homicides, infringements of prisoner's rights and a high-profile escape of six violent inmates. The subsequent investigation into events at this prison suggested that many of the problems could be directly linked to the size of the facility (1700 inmates—just 200 more than Ontario's new mega-jails) and the fact that it was run privately (Office of the Corrections Trustee 1998). In fact, Ohio's experience with such institutions was so egregious, Robert Hagan, then Senator of Ohio, wrote to former Premier Mike Harris cautioning him against Ontario's plans to erect private mega-prisons. In light of such preliminary evidence, many elements of the OCRP initiative are expensive, counterintuitive and ill-advised given that international correctional research clearly shows that coercive approaches to crime rarely, if ever, affect recidivism.

Correctional Institutions, Detention Centres and Punishing for Profit

There are three central themes in Ontario's new "get-tough" approach to punishment.

Correctional Institutions
The correctional policy introduced by the Ontario government in 1996 intends to create a "modernized" correctional system, regularly exercising the slogan of creating "safe, secure, efficient and effective" corrections with "no frills" (OMCS 2000). This policy puts in place virtually every element of new-right criminal justice (privatization, decreasing parole, work programs, mega jails) while systematically ignoring the realities and contradictions plaguing these sorts of correctional initiatives.

One of the most significant initiatives currently underway is the Adult Infrastructure Renewal Project (AIRP). This project, justified by claims of an inefficient and decaying system, plans the closure of approximately twenty correctional facilities, detention centres and jails, the expansion and "modernization" of the remaining facilities and the construction of two new prisons.

Under the AIRP, 1969 beds are being added to four different correctional facilities, transforming one of them (Maplehurst) into a 1500-bed "mega-jail." In addition to this expansion, construction of two entirely new mega-jails is now complete. The prisons in Penetanguishene (The Central North Correctional Facility) and The Central East Correctional Facility (in Lindsay), while fully erected, have yet to open. The Penetanguishene site is scheduled to begin taking prisoners in the fall of 2001. Lindsay, while already having transfers assigned there, doesn't have a clear opening date. Both of these maximum-security facilities follows an identical, panoptic design in which groups of 192 inmates are housed together in sparse concrete pods, each of which houses its own admissions and discharge, visiting room, programming rooms and recreation area.

They also allow for optimal visual surveillance with minimal staff. In mega-jails (including the ones now being constructed in Ontario) one or two guards are stationed in a central control tower from which all of the areas are either clearly visible or monitored by closed-circuit video surveillance. The guards control all doors from the tower, eliminating the need to have guards patrolling ranges or controlling inmate movement through keyed doors. These large capacity prisons are widely used in the U.S.

because of their ability to provide ample space in which to house offenders at the least possible cost.

The mega-jail is the embodiment of the rhetoric of get-tough efficiency and heralds most clearly the end of the rehabilitative and noncarceral eras of corrections in Ontario. The structure of the mega-jail facilitates efficiency, not rehabilitation, and access to rehabilitative programming is limited and restricted. Those incarcerated in such veritable warehouses are rendered unknowable due to the high numbers of inmates and low numbers of staff. Humanity is removed and replaced by technology. This move away from individualizing prisoners and facilitating human interaction is counterintuitive to rehabilitation. The mega-jail, instead, subscribes to a retributive notion of punishment, where offenders are sent to prison not as punishment but rather to be punished. According to this logic, if the costs and pains of imprisonment are accentuated, then the "rational offender" will choose not to return and be deterred from continuing a life of crime.

The move in Ontario towards centralized and homogenous megaprisons replacing smaller institutions dispersed across the province also dismisses earlier trends towards gender and cultural sensitivity. Provincially sentenced women in Ontario will be housed in separate units located within larger male facilities at Maplehurst and Thunder Bay Correctional Centres. The centralization of women's corrections co-located in a large men's prison is in direct opposition to the federal government's approach to women's prisons. This initiative fails on all counts to even remotely reflect the principles of the report of the Women's Issues Task Force. The new unit requires women to be housed on ranges in cells with solid doors with small meal slots. As well, there are minimal provisions for recreation beyond a small, enclosed concrete patio. This is contrasted with the current women's prison in Brampton (slated to be transformed into a boot camp for young offenders), in which women are housed in cottage-style units with large recreational and program facilities.

The female unit at Maplehurst, however, has been able to retain or gain (depending how you see it) more programming and social services. It is designed slightly differently than the male unit largely because of strong advocacy and some bureaucratic support from practitioners and advocates committed to the ideas of women-sensitive correctional models and to the development of alternatives to incarceration for the vast majority of women, who do not pose a "risk" to public safety. However, these changes are small victories. Modifications to this unit are being further compromised by a short-sighted backlash from men's corrections—

which perceives women inmates as being treated preferentially and being given better services.

The new mega-jail presents grave concerns for women in terms of geographic dislocation. The jail is located in a small rural community with limited transportation forty-five minutes away from Toronto. The remoteness of the jail raises a number of concerns, including access to legal counsel; access to court and the increased use of video testimony; access to families (particularly children); availability and access to volunteers; and reintegration/release planning.

The mega-jails are similarly insensitive to the needs of minority inmates. Countering the so-called "club-fed" approach, the provincial mega-jails do not allow space for the construction of sweat lodges or other sites of spiritual importance to a significant number of inmates. The assumption underlying the mega-jail is that offenders are a homogenous mass among which the government appears either unable or unwilling to note differences. Some have speculated that the failure to seriously consider gender as well as racial and ethno-cultural concerns at the new female unit in Milton will recreate a climate of apathy, neglect and discrimination that has historically plagued the Canadian correctional experiences of women and minorities (Haq 1999). Not surprisingly, the new mega strategy is not accompanied by a mega community reintegration plan, which in terms of efficiency and prevention is a significant oversight, given that the average provincially sentenced offender is only in custody for four months and then returned to the community with little support and likely greater disdain for the "system."

Detention Centres
Significant changes have also been effected in the province's detention centres. In 1997, as part of the mandate to develop an efficient "no frills" system of punishment, the Ontario government cut virtually all programming at detention centres. Where inmates used to have access to recreational, life skills, educational, social and work-related programming, now all except those deemed to have special needs have extremely limited access to programs offered only by volunteers. As a result, inmates remain locked down in their cells anywhere from sixteen to twenty-three and a half hours a day and have no access to existing facilities, such as the gymnasium, within the detention centre. The only recreation time made available is the legislatively mandated twenty minutes of outdoor recreation that takes place in a dirty asphalt courtyard. Because of the loss of recreation officers, inmates have no access to even the most basic athletic equipment during

their so-called recreation time. In the time spent out of their cells inmates are confined to their units, enclosed living areas bordering each cell block that consist of picnic-style tables bolted to the floor and a television that may or may not work.

These changes in the daily routines of the detention centres have had serious effects on the overall levels of safety and security at these facilities. Guards we spoke with claim that, since these changes were effected in July of 2000, the overall levels of prison violence have increased significantly in both frequency and severity. Much of this increase is attributed to the loss of programming. It is also suggested that the province's move to make all prisons and detention centres non-smoking by the end of 2000 has had a major impact on inmate temperament, as prisoners are forced to withdraw from nicotine with limited access to the many smoking cessation products currently available.

For those on remand (in custody, awaiting trial), such conditions can have an impact on the decisions they make about their cases and the quality of legal representation. The remand prisoners who are seen as unpredictable are the target of the most oppressive policies, yet many of these offenders are waiting trial and legally innocent of all wrongdoing until proven otherwise.

The loss of programming in the detention centres makes available a good deal of space through the closure of the gymnasiums. A budget of approximately four million dollars is allocated to retrofit the gymnasiums at four of the detention centres, turning them into dormitories for individuals serving intermittent sentences. Through these retrofits, approximately eighty beds will be added to each of these four facilities. One correctional official raised concerns about the ability of the existing gymnasium at Metro East to safely accommodate such a large number of inmates. Having to fit the room not only with eighty beds but also with sufficient showers and toilets to accommodate that number of people will likely create a multitude of visual obstructions, posing real safety concerns to those attempting to patrol it with limited staff availability due to ministry cuts.

The detention centre initiatives follow the same rhetoric as that of correctional centres. Again what is revealed is a sparse, violent and cold environment that invokes images of deprivation and suffering, precisely what a retributive and deterrence-based prison should achieve. The Ontario government is careful, however, not to allow their new correctional narrative to be reduced to raw vengeance. Rather than promoting these changes as harsher punishment, the government very astutely adopted a more business-like response that favours fiscal efficiency as a primary justification for change.

The government's scheme extends beyond the infrastructure of Ontario's prisons to the penal practices within the province. Prisoners are now expected to bear the cost of their own incarceration through prisoner-work programs in which they are taught skills of questionable value, such as how to pick up trash on the highway. Upon entry to prison, inmates have their heads shaved and are stripped of even minor personal effects such as jewelry. In the new order, these practices are intended to build self-esteem. For the inevitable prison violence that will ensue, a zero-tolerance policy has been adopted. Inmates are also being subjected to a mandatory random drug-test scheme. Also underway are increased surveillance and tighter restrictions on parole as well as the reinstatement of militaristic identifiers of rank (new uniforms) and authority (painting lines on the floor for prisoners to wait and walk on) to elicit respect from defiant prisoners. Politicians present all of these symbolic initiatives to the public as if they were rational, efficient and newly improved methods that respond to a manufactured crisis, which threatens the legitimacy of the government in terms of its ability to "fight crime" and protect the public. The get-tough metaphors and strategies evoked by the Ontario government reflect more than a neo-conservative rationality of deterrence; they are also a newly configured rationality of retribution that is designed at its most basic level to simply humiliate and "get even" with the prisoner.

Punishing for Profit

Change also includes extending correctional practice beyond the Ministry of Correctional Services. Perhaps one of the Ontario government's most contentious initiatives with regards to the plan for correctional change is the privatization of correctional institutions and services. Privatization will ensure that punishment remains confined within prison walls, changing only the agents of punishment. The government (OMCS 2000) packages its bid to privatize, stating that:

> building on the success of our partnerships in delivering correctional services, including Project Turnaround and open custody residences, the Ministry of Correctional Services is pursuing alternative service delivery. This involves forming partnerships with service agencies, in either the public or private sector, which can contribute their expertise to the ministry in delivering the most up to date, secure, efficient and effective services.

Project Turnaround, the government's first foray into penal privatization, was the site of a successful escape attempt on the day it opened. Far from claiming the resounding success of Project Turnaround (PT), a summary of the most recent assessments of the facility written by the Ministry's own staff concludes that, "it is premature to determine the impact of PT on young offender recidivism" (Wormith et al. 2001). While the report suggests that, using the Ministry's own measures, Project Turnaround is a success, it fails to attribute this success to the fact that the facility is privately run.

Despite the questionable accomplishments of the government's first attempt at privatizing (and the controversy surrounding private punishment in both Europe and North America), the government is now committed to contracting out the day-to-day operations of the new correctional facility in Penetanguishene. Likely because of the ample and well-substantiated concerns that have been raised about private prisons over the last few years, the Ontario government has exercised extreme caution, avoiding any long-term or intractable commitment to privatization of adult facilities. Instead, it proposes a five-year study of privatization, using Penetanguishene as the test site. The mega-jail currently under construction in Lindsay is meant to act as the control in this experiment, supposedly mirroring Penetanguishene in every way except for the fact that Lindsay, for now, will not be privatized. After the five-year study has been completed, a decision will be made to either return Penetanguishene to public control or, presumably, to privatize first Lindsay and then other facilities. The current contract with Management and Training Corporation (the organization now running Penetanguishene) allows the government to renew for an additional year on the same terms and opt for a second five-year term contingent on renegotiated finances.

Again, the move to privatize the prison at Penetanguishene is being packaged with the government's rubric of get-tough efficiency. The "efficiency" section of the Request For Qualifications (RFQ) is by far the most substantial piece of the first section of the document. Among the greatest inefficiencies of the existing adult correctional system identified in the RFQ are the so-called frills of the Adult Institutional Service Programs like hot meals, functional recreation equipment, counsellors, teachers and social workers and staffing at provincial facilities. These are identified as priority cost-cutting areas in the RFQ.

The underlying assumption on the part of the government is that privatization presents the very real opportunity to create a safe yet more economical penal system. Citing the alleged success of Project Turnaround, the government situates the "development of partnerships as central to assist[ing] the Province in its goal to reach an appropriate balance of detention, correction and accountability." This is despite the reservations expressed by the previous Minister of Correctional Services, Bob Runciman (Canadian Press), in 1998: "there are a whole range of issues around privatization that have not been properly addressed, and public safety is number one. There were some issues raised in the United States recently regarding private operations that raised a number of concerns." In this same speech, Runciman also clearly states that the new correctional facilities (then beginning construction) would *not* be privately run.

The Ministry's complete turnaround not even two years later indicates how little thought has actually been put into the idea of privatization. There is no indication that the government paid proper attention to the concerns raised by Runciman and others, not only about the incident at Youngstown but also about the overall efficacy and utility of privatization. While, as the government notes in the RFQ, there is some evidence indicating that privately run correctional facilities can in fact provide at least as good a level of service as their public counterparts while also cutting costs, there is equally compelling evidence indicating exactly the opposite. Studies of privatization have shown that profit often comes at the cost of adequate correctional care (Nathan 2000). Private facilities consistently have difficulties with under-trained staff, poor quality or non-existent programming, lax security, unclean facilities and sub-standard food and medical care. While the government makes fleeting reference to these issues, it has done little publicly to justify, in light of these concerns, the move towards private corrections in this province.

The bid to privatize Penetanguishene opens opportunity for further discussion of private, for-profit prisons in Ontario. This does not mean that the private sector will displace the government in its role as operator of the justice system. Instead, privatization forwards the new-right agenda of creating a smaller welfare state. Much of the Ontario government's initiatives to date have pivoted on the idea of reducing the government's role in providing a social safety net. The bid to privatize Penetanguishene is well understood as a symbolic (and potentially real) forwarding of this overall agenda. It makes apparent the decreasing government role in any sort of public welfare while ensuring that the government maintains overall control of justice initiatives.

Willful Nostalgia through "Correctional Renewal"?

The entire initiative of get-tough efficiency is consistently characterized by the Ontario government as promoting correctional renewal. Juxtaposing this notion of correctional renewal with the 1980s ideas of correctional reform reveals much about the nature of the Ministry's overall plan. The period leading up to the 1990s is well characterized as an age of correctional reform. When an arena of government is being re-formed, there is an assumption that progressive changes are being effected that will re-work the existing structures into something better and more functional. When the OMCS was engaged in the project of reforming the correctional system in the 1980s the agenda was quite clearly one that intended to create a new and different correctional system, progressing beyond what had already been accomplished within the realm of corrections in the province.

The Ontario government has chosen a project of renewal instead of reform. This phraseology indicates a very different direction for change. The notion of renewal, while still calling for something different than that which has come before, relies on the assumption that there once was something desirable that can now be revived. When we speak of renewing we speak of reclaiming that which has been lost. Renewal then is about regression not progression. Ontario's Correctional Renewal Project conjures up the notion that we can return to an era in corrections where punishment was more straightforward. People committed crimes and were sent to prison where they received harsh treatment until they were released. The problem with Ontario's vision of renewal is that this model never really existed. The effective "deterrent" system Ontario is harkening back to—one in which inmates had their heads shaved, were denied programming, were warehoused in massive, impersonal facilities, were denied parole as a matter of policy, were offered only cold food and were incarcerated hundreds of kilometers from where they live—is a myth.

In his examination of the rise of the boot-camp prison in the U.S. (a prison model that has also found its way to Ontario), Jonathan Simon (1995) observes the presence of a willful nostalgia in contemporary penal rhetoric. The Correctional Renewal Project clearly uses this notion of willful nostalgia. This attempt to revive an era that never existed is clearly more about selling a palatable and popular response to crime to the public than it is about creating a safe, secure, efficient and effective correctional system. The past that has been cobbled together through the OMCS correctional rhetoric draws on these two central mantras of crime control in the new millennium: cutting costs while getting tough. The Ministry relies on popular conceptions of the way prison apparently used to be. What comes to mind when reading any of the Ministry's policy documents are black and white images of prisoners marching in lock-step wearing black and white stripped uniforms, heads shaven, known only by their numbers. This image is appealing on an emotive level, particularly when we are told that these prisons will be run with the greatest efficiency.

What we are left with in terms of corrections in Ontario is not a program of renewal but instead a program of willful regression in which gains that the practice of punishment made over the last few decades are being quickly erased. In this bid to be more fiscally responsible and increasingly punitive, corrections in Ontario is undergoing a devolution that is no longer sensitive to the gendered, racial and spiritual differences among prisoners and is no longer concerned with attempting to devise a set of effective and best practices for the project of rehabilitation and correction. We in Ontario are being brought back to a myth of corrections, an emotional tale in which vengeance and frugality breed safety and reduce criminality. We know that what happens in fairy tales never occurs in reality. The same can be said now for the project of corrections in Ontario.

Notes

1. For a detailed discussion and analysis of the notion of cruelty see Simon 2001.
2. The principle of lesser eligibility followed a deterrence model of punishment whereby prisoners were intended to be kept in conditions worse than the least privileged members of society.
3. A more detailed analysis of supermax prisons can be located in the 2001 issues of the journal *Punishment and Society*.

References

Canadian Press. 1998. October 27.

Commission on Systemic Racism in the Ontario Criminal Justice System (CSROCJS). 1994. *Racism Behind Bars: Interim Report.* Toronto: Queen's Printer for Ontario.

_____. 1995. *Report of the Commission on Systemic Racism in the Ontario Criminal Justice System.* Toronto: Queen's Printer for Ontario.

Garland, D. 2001 *The Culture Of Control: Crime And Social Order In Contemporary Society.* Chicago: University of Chicago Press.

Gendreau, P., P. Smith and C. Goggin. 2000. "Treatment Programs in Corrections." In J. Winterdyk (ed.), *Corrections In Canada.* Toronto: Prentice Hall

Canada.

Haq, R. 1999 "Ontario's Regressive Approach to Prisons: The Negative Impact of Super Jails on Women and their Children." *Canadian Women's Studies* 19(1&2).

Kellough, G. 1996 "Getting Bail: Ideology in Action." In T. Flemming (ed.), *Post Critical Criminology.* Toronto: Prentice Hall.

MacKenzie, Doris-Layton, Robert Brame and David McDowall. 1995. "Boot Camp Prisons and Recidivism in Eight States." *Criminology* 33(3).

McMahon, M. 1992. *Persistent Prison? Rethinking Decarceration and Penal Reform.* Toronto: University of Toronto Press.

Nathan, Stephen. 2000. *Private Adult Correctional Facilities: Fines, Failures and Dubious Practices.* Report. Toronto: Ontario Public Service Employees Union. Available at www.opseu.org/ops/ministry/report/index.htm

Office of the Corrections Trustee for the District of Columbia. 1998. *Inspection and Review of the Northeast Ohio Correctional Centre: Report to the Attorney General.*

Oliver, P. 1992. "Reforming Reform Institutions." In K. McCormick and L. Visano (eds.), *Canadian Penology.* Toronto: Canadian Scholars' Press.

Ontario Ministry of Correctional Services (OMCS). 2000. "Modernization of Jails Puts Public Safety First." Press Release. In Elizabethtown Township. May 5.

Petrosino, Anthony, Carolyn Turpin-Petrosino and James Finckenauer. 2000. "Well-meaning Programs can have Harmful Effects! Lessons from Experiments of Programs such as Scared Straight." *Crime and Delinquency* 46(3).

Simon, J. 2001. "Entitlement to Cruelty: The End of Welfare and the Punitive Mentality in the United States." In K. Stenson and R. Sullivan (eds.), *Crime, Risk and Justice.* Cullompton, U.K.: Willan Publishing.

_____. 1995. "They Died With Their Boots On: The Boot Camp and the Limits of Modern Penality." *Social Justice* 22(2).

Spirenburg, Peter. 1984. *The Spectacle of Suffering: Executions and the Evolution of Repression: From a Preindustrial Metropolis to the European Experience.* London: Cambridge University Press.

Winterdyk, J. 2000. *Corrections in Canada.* Toronto: Prentice Hall Canada.

Wormith, Stephen, Jeffrey Wright, Isabelle Sauve and Paul Fleury. 2001. *Ontario's Strict Discipline Facility is not just Another "Boot Camp" Report.* encourageyouth.ca. September 9.

Women's Issues Task Force (WITF). 1993. *Women's Voices, Women's Choices.* Toronto: Ontario Ministry of Correctional Services.